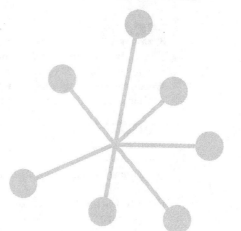

HOW TO
Plan
Rigorous Instruction

ROBYN R. JACKSON

ASCD
Alexandria, Virginia USA

mindsteps
Washington, DC

1703 N. Beauregard St. • Alexandria, VA 22311-1714 USA
Phone: 800-933-2723 or 703-578-9600 • Fax: 703-575-5400
Website: www.ascd.org • E-mail: member@ascd.org
Author guidelines: www.ascd.org/write

mindsteps™

Washington, DC
Phone: 888-565-8881
Website: www.mindstepsinc.com

Gene R. Carter, *Executive Director;* Judy Zimny, *Chief Program Development Officer,* Nancy Modrak, *Publisher;* Scott Willis, *Director, Book Acquisitions & Development;* Genny Ostertag, *Acquisitions Editor;* Julie Houtz, *Director, Book Editing & Production;* Katie Martin, *Editor;* Reece Quiñones, *Senior Graphic Designer;* Mike Kalyan, *Production Manager;* Barton Matheson Willse & Worthington, *Typesetter*

All web links in this book are correct as of the publication date below but may have become inactive or otherwise modified since that time. If you notice a deactivated or changed link, please e-mail books@ascd.org with the words "Link Update" in the subject line. In your message, please specify the web link, the book title, and the page number on which the link appears.

PAPERBACK ISBN: 978-1-4166-1093-9   ASCD product #110077   n1/11

Quantity discounts for the paperback edition only: 10–49 copies, 10%; 50+ copies, 15%; for 1,000 or more copies, call 800-933-2723, ext. 5634, or 703-575-5634. For desk copies: member@ascd.org.

Library of Congress Cataloging-in-Publication Data

Jackson, Robyn Renee, author.
    How to plan rigorous instruction / Robyn R. Jackson.
        p. cm.
    Includes bibliographical references and index.
    ISBN 978-1-4166-1093-9 (pbk. : alk. paper)
    1. Curriculum planning.   2. Lesson planning.   3. Education—Standards.
4. Critical thinking.   5. Effective teaching.   I. Title.
    LB2806.15.J28 2011
    371.3028—dc22   2010044052

20 19 18 17 16 15 14 13   3 4 5 6 7 8 9 10 11 12

MASTERING
THE PRINCIPLES OF GREAT
TEACHING

How to Plan Rigorous Instruction

About the Mastering the Principles of Great Teaching Series 1

How to Use This Guide 4

Self-Assessment: Knowing Where Your Students Are Going 9

Introduction: Understanding the Mastery Principle 13

If we want all our students to become better thinkers and learners, we must design rigorous learning experiences that go beyond helping them simply master standards.

1. **Creating a Rigorous Unit Assessment** 22

   How will you know whether students have met a standard in a highly rigorous way? The first step is to select or create a rigorous unit assessment to guide your instruction.

2. **Selecting Rigorous Learning Material** 40

   Once you have created a rigorous summative assessment for a unit, what content will foster the kind of thinking and learning necessary for mastery? The next step is to identify the rigorous learning material that will be the basis for your instruction.

3. **Choosing Rigorous Instructional Strategies**..57

Now that you have your learning material set, which instructional strategies will you use to move students toward rigorous mastery of your standards and objectives? Your next task is to plan rigorous learning experiences.

4. **Putting It All Together** 92

You've spent time thinking through rigorous assessment, content, and instructional strategies. Now it's time to put it all together and create a rigorous learning unit.

Conclusion...104

Appendixes 107

References...119

About the Author 120

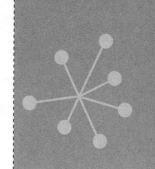

About the Mastering the Principles of Great Teaching Series

Have you ever wondered what it takes to become a master teacher? Sure, you know what master teachers do—what their classrooms look like, how they structure their lessons, the kinds of assessments they give, and the strategies they use. But becoming a master teacher involves more than simply doing what master teachers do. To be a master teacher, you need to *think* like a master teacher.

If you ask master teachers their secret, they may not be able to tell you. That's because most master teachers have a difficult time explaining what makes them masterful in the classroom. Much of what they do in the classroom feels automatic, fluid, and natural. To them, their mastery is simply *teaching*.

How did they get so good? How did they become master teachers, and how can you become one yourself? The answer is that master teachers have learned how to rigorously apply a few simple principles of great teaching to their practice. They have, in short, developed a master teacher mindset.

The seven principles of mastery teaching are

1. Start where your students are.
2. Know where your students are going.
3. Expect to get your students to their goal.
4. Support your students along the way.

5. Use feedback to help you and your students get better.

6. Focus on quality rather than quantity.

7. Never work harder than your students.

As you can see, none of these principles is particularly earth shattering. They are things we all know intuitively that we should be doing in the classroom. But the master teacher mindset develops as a result of systematically and rigorously applying these principles to teaching until they become our spontaneous response to our students. The more you practice these principles, the more you too can begin to think like a master teacher, and the closer you will come to having a master teacher mindset.

How can you start to practice these principles in your own classroom? How can you do so in a way that is true to your own style and suits the learning needs of your particular students? How, in other words, can you systematically apply mastery principles to address the everyday challenges you face as a teacher? This series will show you what to do.

If you discovered this series through its companion book, *Never Work Harder Than Your Students and Other Principles of Great Teaching* (Jackson, 2009), you'll find some familiar concepts covered here. While *Never Work Harder Than Your Students* introduced the principles of mastery teaching, the how-to guides in the Mastering the Principles of Great Teaching series will take you step-by-step through the process of integrating those principles into your classroom practice and show you how to apply the principles to resolve specific teaching challenges you face.

Each of the how-to guides in this series focuses on one of the seven mastery principles. You'll examine the principle, assess your current practice of the principle, and learn new ways to incorporate it in your teaching. And because the series is designed to show the mastery principles in relation to specific teaching challenges, working your way through each guide will help you to resolve many of your immediate, day-to-day classroom challenges even as you build your overall mastery mindset.

Mastery teaching is not about fitting into a specific mold, and these guides are designed to help you grow no matter where you are in your practice. If you have read *Never Work Harder Than Your Students*, you may recall that it includes a diagnostic tool to help teachers assess their skill-level in each principle and locate themselves along a mastery teaching continuum ranging from novice to apprentice to practitioner to master teacher. Each of the how-to guides in this series also begins with a diagnostic tool to help you identify where you fall on the continuum so that you can focus specifically on the strategies best suited to your current practice. This format ensures that you will be able to work through all the guides at your own pace and level, cycle back through, and, with each rereading, deepen your understanding and further the development of your master teacher mindset.

The guides in the Mastering the Principles of Great Teaching series follow a standard format. After an introduction to the focus mastery principle and the diagnostic, you will work through chapters that prompt you to apply the principle rigorously and systematically to your classroom practice. Along the way, you will learn new strategies, develop new skills, and take time to reflect on your growth. The tools in each guide help you take a close look at your own teaching, examine your assumptions about teaching and how students learn, and refine your instruction so that your students can learn more effectively.

Becoming a master teacher has little to do with how many years you put in or how closely you resemble a particular Hollywood ideal. It isn't some special gift doled out at birth to only a chosen few. Any teacher can become a master teacher with the right kind of practice—the kind of practice this series of how-to guides offers. In working through them, you too can develop a master teacher mindset and be the master teacher your students deserve.

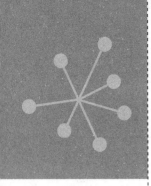

How to Use This Guide

Let's face it. In the real world, our lesson plans rarely look like the carefully crafted, double-spaced, neatly typed plans we handed in to our professors. Once we got into the classroom, our plans soon become agendas scribbled in a plan book, notes written in the pages of a textbook, or daily outlines carried around in our heads. Formal lesson planning is a nice idea in theory, but most of us are too busy to fill out the forms, complete the templates, or create the five-page document that many lesson formats demand.

What's more, lesson planning in today's environment seems more about proving that we have covered the material on state tests than it does about dreaming up exciting and innovative ways to help students learn. And yet, there is merit in taking time to plan robust learning experiences for students. Doing so allows you to create lessons that are much more focused, activities that are more relevant and engaging, and assessments that are much more informative to both you and your students. You can help your students go beyond a surface understanding of the material and see the connection between what they are doing in class and their ultimate learning goals.

Focusing on the mastery principle "Know Where Your Students Are Going," this how-to guide will show you a way to plan rigorous learning units from start to finish—regardless of the grade level or discipline you teach. Not only will you learn an effective way to plan lessons that will prepare your students to succeed on summative tests, you'll also learn how to help students become critical thinkers, effective problem solvers, and reflective learners. In doing so, you can go beyond the limitations of your curriculum and move from what has been prescribed for your students to what is truly possible for them.

How This Guide Is Structured

How to Plan Rigorous Instruction begins with an **Introduction** to the mastery principle and a **Self-Assessment**—a diagnostic tool to help you identify where your current application of the principle "Know Where Your Students Are Going" falls on the continuum of mastery teaching. Then, it's on to the guide's four chapters, each corresponding to a stage in the process for developing a rigorous learning unit:

- **Chapter 1: Creating Rigorous Unit Assessments** shows you how to plan and construct or select rigorous summative assessments that will provide a starting point for a rigorous learning unit.

- **Chapter 2: Selecting Rigorous Learning Materials** helps you determine whether the content you are using is rigorous. You will learn how to increase the level of rigor in your lessons by selecting content that is ambiguous, is complex, is layered, and has implicit meaning.

- **Chapter 3: Choosing Rigorous Instructional Strategies** helps you ensure that students engage with the content you have chosen in a highly rigorous way. You will learn how to move students systematically through the stages of rigorous learning so that they build their capacity for rigorous thinking. And you will learn specific instructional strategies that promote rigorous engagement.

- **Chapter 4: Putting It All Together** shows you how to combine rigorous assessments, content, and instructional strategies into a highly rigorous unit plan.

Throughout the guide, **Your Turn** sections provide suggestions for how you can begin to take action in your own classroom. These suggestions are divided into four levels, keyed to your current level of principle application:

- *Acquire.* The suggestions here are designed to help those working at the novice level develop a better understanding of the principle and of their own teaching practice as it relates to the principle.

- *Apply.* The suggestions here focus on showing those working at the apprentice level how to use the guide's strategies to improve their teaching practice.

- **Assimilate.** The suggestions here are designed to give those working at the practitioner level additional ideas about how to incorporate the principle and strategies into their existing practice.

- **Adapt.** The suggestions here will help those working at the master teacher level take a fresh look at their own practice and customize some of the guide's strategies in a way that's right for them and their students.

Think of this guide like a spiral staircase in which you return to the same concepts more than once, each time pushing yourself to an incrementally higher level as you proceed toward mastery. The breaks between each level are natural "rest stops"—places where you will know you've made substantial progress and can pause so that you won't feel overwhelmed or stuck before moving forward. Rest assured, even if you don't move beyond the *Acquire* suggestions your first time through the guide, you will still have made progress. Stop there and try those skills out in your classroom. Then, as your ability and confidence grow, you can return with the next unit in mind. Each time you will continue enhancing your practice by ramping up to the apprentice level and beyond as you build your master teacher mindset and refine your practice.

Tools

Within each section, you'll also find other tools to help you reach your goals, including

 Checklists outlining what you will accomplish at each step.

 Time-Saving Tips to steer you toward information that will allow you to complete each step more quickly.

 Checkpoint Summaries that quickly summarize some of the main concepts in this guide. You can use these to assess your own understanding of specific concepts and as a handy reminder of some of the key points.

 Take It Step by Step boxes that summarize the key steps in a process and serve as handy reminders later on.

Learn More Online sections that point you to other strategies and additional resources available on the web.

 Think About sections that raise reflection questions designed to prompt you to consider what you've read and make connections to your own classroom and teaching practice.

 Yes, But . . . sections addressing common objections and reservations teachers sometimes express in relation to these strategies. These sections will help you resolve some practical challenges and overcome any hesitation you might be feeling.

You will also find a variety of worksheets, planning templates, and strategy sheets that will help you capture your learning and build a comprehensive plan. The **Appendixes** at the end of the guide highlight developmentally appropriate rigorous learning practices and offer support for matching rigorous instructional approaches to instructional goals.

Your Approach

If you are working through this how-to guide individually, first take time to understand the book's general framework. Preview the material and make a commitment to spend a certain amount of time each week working through the various steps. You can read through the book entirely before deciding where to begin, or you can jump right in and start trying some of the strategies outlined. Either way, be sure to reflect periodically on how applying these strategies affects your practice and your students. Then, adjust your practice accordingly.

If you are working through this book with other teachers in a small-group setting, begin with an overview of the various steps in the process and discuss which steps might give each group member the most trouble and in which steps members of your group might have some expertise. Use this information to designate a group facilitator for each step in order to keep everyone focused and on track. Then make a commitment as a group about how you will work through the steps individually, and meet regularly to discuss your progress, share your triumphs, and brainstorm ways around your challenges. You can use the "Think About" sections as a starting point for group discussion and then share individual strategies that you have implemented in the classroom.

If you are an administrator or teacher leader, this book will give you an overview of the rigorous learning that should be happening in every classroom. And it will provide you with useful tools you can offer to teachers as you conference with them and support their professional development. The Appendixes include several tools you can use to support and monitor a teacher's use of rigorous instruction in the classroom.

Share Your Progress

As always, we want to hear from you! Contact us at info@mindstepsinc.com to ask questions, share your experiences, and pass along success stories of how you've made a difference in supporting struggling students. Administrators and district-level leaders are welcome to contact us to learn more about the supports Mindsteps Inc. offers for teachers and schools; give us a call at 1-888-565-8881, e-mail us at info@mindstepsinc. com, or visit us on the web at www.mindstepsinc.com.

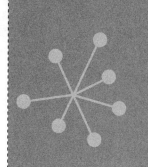

Self-Assessment:
Knowing Where Your Students Are Going

Answer each of the following questions as honestly as you can; don't think about what you would like to do but about what you currently do in your own practice. There are no right or wrong answers.

1. When I am faced with a new curriculum, I usually
   a. Figure out how I will cover all the material in each unit and start creating lesson plans.
   b. Use the lesson plans included in the curriculum guide.
   c. Look at the assessment and "back map" from there.
   d. Start with the standards and use them to create learning objectives.

2. When I look at the curriculum standards, the first thing I do is
   a. Figure out what assessments I will use so that I will know when my students have mastered the standards.
   b. Figure out which assignments and activities will best help my students meet the standards.
   c. Figure out how I am going to teach all the standards in the time I have.
   d. Figure out how the lesson objectives in the curriculum guide match up against the standards.

3. When I write objectives, I usually
   a. Try to state them using the wording favored by the district.

b. Figure out and then list the activities I want my students to complete.

c. Figure out and then list the concepts and skills I want my students to master.

d. Figure out what I want my students to learn and then how I can communicate this in a way that students will understand.

4. When it comes to summative assessment, I generally

a. Write my own test, usually after I have taught the unit.

b. Write my own test after I have planned the unit and have a sense of the material I will be able to cover.

c. Write my own test before I plan the unit.

d. Use the test included in the curriculum guide.

5. When selecting learning materials, I generally

a. Choose materials that will best help my students exercise the thinking skills and processes the unit demands.

b. Choose materials based on my students' interests and skills.

c. Use the materials recommended by the curriculum guide.

d. Supplement the materials recommended in the curriculum guide with those I believe will be more interesting to my students.

6. When planning learning experiences for students, the typical pathway to mastery I set is

a. Lesson objective, activator, lesson, summarizer, summative assessment.

b. Direct instruction, guided practice, independent practice, summative assessment.

c. Lower-level Bloom's to upper-level Bloom's.

d. Understanding, thinking skills, thinking processes, habits of mind.

7. I believe students learn best when units are planned

a. In a linear fashion, with a direct pathway to mastery.

b. In an episodic fashion, where students reach points of mastery.

c. In a cyclical fashion, where students revisit earlier material and deepen their understanding.

d. In a step-by-step fashion, where students build mastery and reach higher levels of understanding over time.

8. I know that students are engaged in rigorous learning when

    a. They think in complex, flexible, and resilient ways.

    b. They grapple with complex and challenging material.

    c. They manage multiple assignments and a difficult workload successfully.

    d. They achieve high scores on rigorous summative assessments.

Scoring

For each question, circle the number in the column that represents your answer. For instance, if you answered A for question 1, you would circle the 2. When you have finished, calculate the totals for each column and determine your grand total by adding up the four column totals.

Question	A	B	C	D	
1	2	1	4	3	
2	4	3	1	2	
3	1	2	3	4	
4	2	3	4	1	
5	4	3	1	2	
6	1	2	3	4	
7	1	2	3	4	
8	4	3	1	2	**Grand Total**
Total					

Going Forward

Use your grand total to determine your of current level of principle application and locate the most appropriate suggestions for taking action in your own classroom.

8–11 points: Novice

If you scored in the novice range, focus on the **Acquire** suggestions. If some of the content and practices discussed are familiar, you may wish to jump to the suggestions under the *Apply, Assimilate*, and *Adapt* headings. As you build your confidence with the *Acquire* actions, return to this book and work through it again at a different level.

12–19 points: Apprentice

If you scored in the apprentice range, focus on the ***Apply*** sections. Try some of the strategies in this guide with a small unit of study, and pay attention to how they work for your students and to what feels right to you. As you become more comfortable applying these skills, or if you are already implementing some of the practices in the *Apply* sections, consider the *Assimilate* or *Adapt* suggestions, and look for ways to refine what you are already doing.

20–27 points: Practitioner

If you scored in the practitioner range, focus on the ***Assimilate*** suggestions. Look for ways to begin integrating more of this guide's recommended strategies into your overall practice so that your use of them becomes more automatic and comprehensive. If a particular practice is new to you, start at the *Acquire* or *Apply* suggestions and work your way up to those under *Assimilate*. If a practice is embedded into your teaching habits already, try some suggestions associated with the *Adapt* heading.

28–32 points: Master Teacher

If you scored in the master teacher range, focus on the ***Adapt*** suggestions. Many of the rigorous instructional strategies presented in this guide are already a part of your classroom philosophy and practice. Your goal should be to customize the *Adapt* suggestions to your students and your classroom context. If you come across a strategy that is new to you, take time to work through the *Acquire, Adapt*, and *Assimilate* suggestions so that it too can become a seamless part of your overall practice.

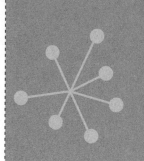

Introduction:
Understanding the Mastery Principle

If we want *all* our students to become better thinkers and learners, we must design rigorous learning experiences that go beyond helping them simply master standards.

In *Never Work Harder Than Your Students*, I noted that master teachers see the standards of the courses we teach as the "final destination" for classroom instruction. Standards represent where our students need to go, and by unpacking standards into essential questions and smaller objectives, we can plan the learning experiences that will get students where they need to be. The tests to which standards are often matched give us concrete ways of determining that students have successfully mastered certain concepts and skills.

However, standards and tests often do a poor job of articulating what we *really* want our students to learn as a result of their time in our classes. If I were to ask you what your hopes and dreams are for your students, chances are you wouldn't reply with "I really want them to be able to multiply two-digit numbers accurately and under timed conditions," or "Boy, would I like them to be able to correctly identify synecdoche in a poem." What we want for our students is something loftier: We want them to understand multiplication and be able to use it to solve problems. We want them to appreciate the beauty of poetry.

The mastery principle "Know Where Your Students Are Going" is about more than unpacking the standards and objectives of your curricula. It goes beyond writing essential questions or mastery objectives. Knowing where your students are going requires that you examine *the type of thinking* you want them to engage in, *the type of understanding* you want them to walk away with, and *the type of learners* you hope to help them become. It means setting a destination that's worth working toward, and then carefully planning the lessons that will take students there.

To be honest, it is much easier to think about instruction in terms of tightly scripted objectives handed down by your school or district—and it's a whole lot safer too, given today's test-focused environment. But it's also limiting for both you and your students. It keeps you from understanding and tapping into your students' full potential, and it makes for pretty dry learning experiences for them. What if you could go beyond planning and delivering tightly scripted lessons mapped to a standardized test to facilitate rich, robust learning experiences? What if, instead of just preparing your students to be good test takers, you could also prepare them to be critical thinkers and lifelong learners? What if you didn't have to choose between an interesting and engaging lesson and one that meets the criteria prescribed by your curriculum guide? In other words, what if you could teach creatively, passionately, and freely while helping students meet and exceed the standards of your course?

The good news is that you *can*. Your vision for where your students are going doesn't have to stop at the state test, and your teaching can stretch beyond the barriers of the curriculum guide. You can help your students meet the standards set for your course, pass the big test, *and* become engaged learners, effective problem solvers, and critical thinkers. This guide will show you how.

The chapters ahead focus on how to plan robust, rigorous learning experiences for your students that will help them learn how to think about what they are learning and how to use their learning in meaningful ways. With this approach, your lessons will not only be much more interesting and engaging, but they will also do a better job of preparing students for the challenges they will face once they leave your classroom. And the key to this kind of lesson is *rigor*.

What Is Rigor?

Rigor is one of those slippery concepts in education. Everyone agrees that it is important, and everybody wants standards, instruction, and assessments that are rigorous, but very few agree on what "rigor" really means. In most cases, educators believe that they know rigor when they see it without really having a fully defined idea of what it looks like.

Think of the times you might have used the term "rigorous" to mean a learning task that was "harder" or "more challenging" or "focused on the upper levels of Bloom's taxonomy." While all of these concepts play into rigor, rigor is more than that. So before we begin the work of this how-to guide—planning rigorous learning units—it is important to define what we mean when we talk about rigor in the classroom. Here's a definition we might start with: Rigor is a *quality of instruction* that requires students to "construct meaning and impose structure on situations rather than expect to find them already apparent" (Resnick, 1987, p. 44). Whereas most units work toward what students *will know and be able to do* by the end of instruction, rigorous learning units also ask *what students will understand* and *how students will be able to think*. Rigorous instruction is designed to develop students' capacity to

- Think accurately and with clarity.
- Identify and consider multiple meanings and interpretations.
- Take and support a position.
- Resist impulsivity and engage in disciplined inquiry and thought.
- Work within and outside the bounds of standard conventions, and develop their own standards of evaluation.
- Use and adapt what they know to deal with uncertainty and novelty.
- Adjust their approach when presented with new constraints.
- Tolerate uncertainty and work through ambiguity and complexity.

In short, rigor is quality of instruction that goes beyond helping students memorize facts, acquire an understanding of concepts, and develop basic skill proficiency. Rigorous instruction asks students to create their own meaning, integrate skills into processes, and use what they have learned to solve real-world problems, even when the "correct" answer is unclear and they are faced with perplexing unknowns.

Why Rigor?

The mastery principle "Know Where Your Students Are Going" is about the need to have a clear idea of the point of our instruction. Sure, we have standards we're required to work toward as a part of our curriculum, but unless we unpack those standards and understand the types of learning and comprehension those standards imply, we are missing the point. And if we aren't careful, we can get so caught up marching our students toward mastery that we miss out on helping them experience real learning. If you want your students to master standards in a meaningful and relevant way, rigor is the key.

Rigor is also what makes a learning unit robust, engaging, and appropriately challenging. Lessons designed to be rigorous require students to go beyond a surface understanding of the material. These lessons, by design, foster students' ability to think and learn for themselves.

Here are a few more reasons why rigorous instruction is a valuable pursuit:

- ***Rigor fosters persistence.*** When students must dig for the answers, they discover the value of the search. A little effort leads to small rewards, and more effort over an extended period leads to greater ones.

- ***Rigor fosters resilience.*** When students learn to engage in rigorous thinking and inquiry, they learn how to manage and work through frustration to solve problems on their own. They develop a tolerance for uncertainty, acquire the skills and the disposition to handle struggle, and build a track record of overcoming tough challenges.

- ***Rigor fosters flexibility.*** Rigorous instruction helps students grasp that learning is messy and unpredictable, and that understanding is something to be pursued through multiple pathways that are often complex, layered, and ambiguous.

- ***Rigor fosters purposefulness.*** Students come to see that they are learning in order to make meaning, to broaden their own understanding, and to solve interesting problems.

- ***Rigor fosters metacognition.*** Rigorous instruction asks students to think about their learning goals, select appropriate strategies for pursuing those goals, and reflect on the effectiveness of their chosen approach.

- ***Rigor fosters ownership.*** When students must make meaning for themselves, they come to own what they have learned. Rather than be passive recipients of knowledge, students actively participate in constructing knowledge, filling in unstated information and imposing order on what they are learning.

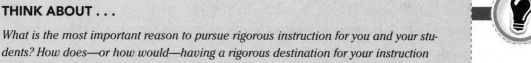

THINK ABOUT . . .

What is the most important reason to pursue rigorous instruction for you and your students? How does—or how would—having a rigorous destination for your instruction change your instructional goals and practices?

Seven Myths About Rigor

Uncertainty over the meaning of rigor in education has led to a number of misconceptions that we ought to address up front.

- *Myth 1: Rigor means more work.* Rigor is about the quality of the work students are asked to do, not the quantity. More assignments or more reading does not guarantee a greater degree of rigor. In fact, rigorous classrooms often have fewer assignments and less homework.

- *Myth 2: Rigor means the work is harder.* Standard dictionary definitions of "rigor" do focus on strictness, severity, and difficulty, so this misinterpretation of educational rigor is understandable. And although it's true that rigorous classrooms do present more challenge to students, there is a difference between what is challenging and what is difficult. Challenging work asks students to stretch and reach for new understanding. In contrast, "difficult" work can be difficult for a variety of reasons, including unclear instructions, a lack of necessary resources, a lack of adequate support, and demands that are too great for the time allotted. We can all think of assignments we endured as students that were difficult but not intellectually challenging. Thus, it is a mistake to think that just because students have difficulty completing their work, they are engaged in a rigorous assignment.

- *Myth 3: If you have rigorous standards, you automatically have a rigorous course.* Rigor isn't as much about the standards as it is about how you ask students to reach the standards. Many teachers and curriculum guides have asked students to achieve highly rigorous standards in unrigorous ways. But teachers have the power to transform mediocre standards into highly rigorous learning by designing rigorous learning experiences.

- *Myth 4: Rigor is a matter of content.* Selecting highly rigorous content does not guarantee a highly rigorous learning experience for students. *How* you ask students to engage in the content is the most powerful determinant of the level of rigor in your classroom.

- ***Myth 5: Younger students cannot engage in rigorous learning.*** Even young children can think and interact with material in highly rigorous ways. In fact, left to their own devices, children naturally take what they are learning to solve unpredictable problems and deal with uncertainty. The key is to make sure that your rigorous instruction is developmentally appropriate. The chart in Appendix A can help you plan these kinds of lessons.

- ***Myth 6: Rigor is only possible after students have mastered the basics.*** Any level of learning can be rigorous if you design the experience to be so. For example, students learning even the most basic material can be asked to build representations, organize facts, analyze and construct relationships among facts, and make inferences beyond what is explicitly presented in class.

- ***Myth 7: Rigor is for the elite.*** To reserve rigorous learning opportunities for an elite group of students while relegating others to lives of memorizing disconnected facts and blindly participating in meaningless activities is to leave the majority of students unprepared to meet the demands of the 21st century and beyond. All students can and should have access to rigorous instruction and learning.

THINK ABOUT . . .

Which of these myths about rigor have shaped your beliefs and practice?

The Truth About Rigor

The truth is, planning and facilitating rigorous learning experiences is one of the most rewarding things you can do as a teacher. Your class discussions are much livelier, your assignments are more interesting, and your students are much more involved in the class. Rigorous lessons allow you the chance to take your students more deeply into your subject and give them the tools they need to learn how to learn for themselves. Here are a few other truths about rigor.

- ***Rigorous instruction asks students to make nuanced judgments.*** There may be several solutions to a problem, each with costs and benefits, and students learn to choose from a range of available options. They consider and apply multiple, sometimes conflicting, criteria and wrestle with shades of meaning in order to come to a solution or a conclusion. And students learn to defend their choices even when there is no clear "right" answer.

- ***Rigorous instruction requires effortful learning.*** Students cannot be passive recipients of knowledge; they must work at learning, make meaning on their own, and impose structure on apparent disorder. While we provide students with proactive support to prevent unproductive struggle, we do give them space to pursue understanding and resolve problems independently.

- ***Rigorous instruction is intentional.*** Students are asked to strategically pursue a learning goal. They must build on prior knowledge and make informed choices. In rigorous classrooms, students are actively engaged in analyzing, synthesizing, and evaluating ideas for themselves.

- ***Rigorous instruction involves uncertainty.*** Not everything that students need to know is readily apparent, and the "right" answer is not always obvious. In fact, there may not be just one right answer at all. And because rigorous instruction asks students to take learning paths that are not tightly scripted, there are times when not even the teacher knows exactly what will happen next. Rigorous instruction asks students to embrace learning as a not-so-tidy process of applying skills and knowledge and adapting them to new situations.

- ***Rigorous instruction builds self-regulation skills.*** It asks students to reflect on and manage the learning process in a strategic and mindful way. They learn how to tell when they are confused, how to select appropriate strategies, how to pace themselves, when and how to ask for help, how to persist through frustration, and how to tell whether they are struggling productively or destructively.

- ***Rigorous instruction is relevant.*** Students don't memorize facts or acquire new skills without also understanding their real-world application. That doesn't mean that every rigorous learning experience results in a direct real-world application, but it does mean that even when students are engaged in simulated activities or practice exercises, they can make the connection between what they are doing and how it might be useful outside the classroom.

- ***Rigorous instruction is relative.*** There is no absolute value for rigor, nor is it inherent in content or in the instructional strategies themselves. Rigorous instruction is within, but at the outer edges of, students' capabilities and helps students to expand what they can do. Rigor is "in reach"—and that reach is different for every student, in each grade level, and within each discipline.

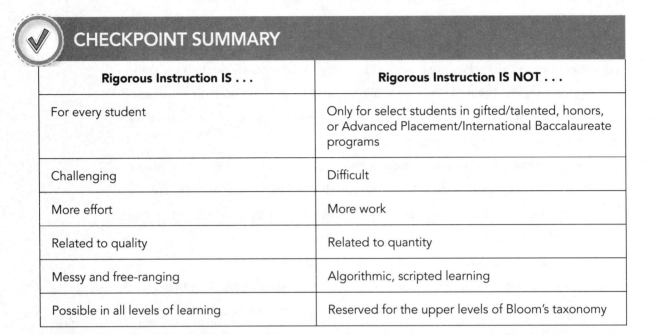

CHECKPOINT SUMMARY

Rigorous Instruction IS . . .	Rigorous Instruction IS NOT . . .
For every student	Only for select students in gifted/talented, honors, or Advanced Placement/International Baccalaureate programs
Challenging	Difficult
More effort	More work
Related to quality	Related to quantity
Messy and free-ranging	Algorithmic, scripted learning
Possible in all levels of learning	Reserved for the upper levels of Bloom's taxonomy

THINK ABOUT . . .

What is your personal definition of rigor in the classroom? How does it align with the definition and characteristics discussed so far? What would you add to or change about the portrait of rigorous instruction presented here?

YOUR TURN

Acquire: After reviewing the characteristics of rigorous instruction listed in the Checkpoint Summary and the truths about rigor discussed on pages 18–20, review the lessons in a unit you teach to see if and how they are "rigorous." What parts of the lesson were rigorous, and what parts were not?

Apply: Think about a unit you will teach in the next two weeks. Review the Checkpoint Summary and the truths about rigor discussed on pages 18–20 and consider how you might adjust your unit plans to reflect your understanding of this material. For instance, you might want to adjust your unit to introduce some uncertainty, or you might include an activity that promotes metacognition. Find at least one way to make your upcoming unit more rigorous.

Assimilate: How are your lessons already rigorous? How might you adjust them to be more rigorous?

Adapt: Think about an entire year's worth of instruction for the course or grade level you teach. How might you adapt your lessons and units to make them more rigorous?

1

Creating a Rigorous
Unit Assessment

In this chapter you will . . .

- [ ] Find out why planning a unit assessment first supports rigorous instruction.
- [ ] Learn the three criteria for a rigorous assessment.
- [ ] Learn the steps to creating a rigorous assessment.
- [ ] Look at the various assessment formats that lend themselves to rigorous assessment.
- [ ] Select or plan a rigorous assessment for an upcoming unit.

Time-Saving Tools

You will complete the work in this chapter more quickly if you have the following handy:

- [ ] Your standards, objectives, and essential questions for an upcoming unit.
- [ ] Any curriculum guides for the unit provided by your school or district.

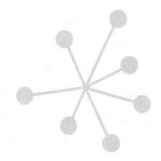

How will you know whether students have met a standard in a highly rigorous way? The first step is to select or create a rigorous unit assessment to guide your instruction.

Few teachers today create their learning standards from scratch; in most cases, the standards for a grade level or course are established by the curriculum, the district, or the state. These standards represent both a starting point and an end point for instruction. As a starting point, they provide direction on the type of learning experiences and materials that will help students engage in the kind of thinking and learning embedded in the standard. As an end point, they establish a level of achievement for you and your students to work toward throughout the year.

This latter issue—the ways that standards operate as an end point for instruction—is first on our agenda. In this chapter, you will learn how to create or select rigorous assessments to best measure how well your students have met the standards. Once you have established a rigorous final assessment, you'll be able to create instructional materials and learning experiences to ensure that your students meet the standards in a highly rigorous way and can demonstrate mastery on these assessments.

YES, BUT . . .

What if my standards aren't rigorous?

Even if you don't consider your standards to be particularly rigorous, you can still set learning goals and select content and learning experiences that will push students to meet these standards in highly rigorous ways. For example, with rigorous learning goals, you might design instruction that not only helps students "understand the difference between a republic and a democracy," as the (rather lackluster) standard requires, but also helps students achieve the higher goal of becoming better citizens. By choosing challenging content and creating lessons that require students to think critically, flexibly, and creatively, you can help them exceed course standards and build their capacity to engage in highly rigorous thinking and learning.

Start Unit Planning with a Rigorous Summative Assessment

Although you are probably accustomed to planning by first consulting the curriculum, then selecting materials and learning experiences, and finally creating a summative assessment, when it comes to planning rigorous learning units, we're actually going to work *backward*. We'll start with a rigorous assessment and then select the learning experiences and materials that will give students the best chance of successfully passing that assessment. This is a good idea for several reasons.

First, starting with the summative assessment is a way to clarify learning goals and pinpoint what it is you really want students to learn. The assessment-first approach helps you decide what constitutes mastery of the learning goals and how you want students to be able to demonstrate that mastery. It also helps you make better choices about *mastery thresholds*—the baseline of goal mastery or the point at which you can safely say that a student is within the range of mastery. Once you're clear about the mastery threshold, you can plan learning experiences that are more effective at helping students reach mastery, and you'll have a better idea of when students are not on track.

Second, starting unit planning with the summative assessment helps you choose appropriate learning experiences for students. Once you really know where students need to go, you can make better, more focused choices about content and instructional strategies and about the ongoing assessments you'll use to monitor and support students' progress throughout the unit.

Let's come right out and say it: An assessment-first approach is indeed about "teaching to the test." That's a notion some people bristle at, and yes, it certainly can feel confining and disheartening to be asked to teach to a "bad" test that emphasizes factual recall over other forms of learning. But when the test is good, teaching toward it makes sense and can give your instruction focus, direction, and clarity. The problem, then, is not teaching to the test but finding or creating a test that's good enough—rigorous enough—to teach toward.

What Makes an Assessment Rigorous?

So what makes a good test? Ultimately, a rigorous assessment measures how well students, when faced with uncertainties, discrepancies, or seemingly irresolvable conundrums, can use what they have learned to develop sound solutions to problems.

A rigorous assessment meets three criteria: (1) It measures thinking skills rather than factual recall, (2) it sustains or reinforces rigorous engagement by asking students to think in highly rigorous ways, and (3) it asks students to apply what they have learned to real-world or unpredictable situations. Let's look at each of the criteria in more detail.

Rigorous Assessments Measure Thinking Skills, Not Factual Recall

Rather than merely require students to accurately reproduce what they have learned, rigorous assessments ask students to take what they have learned and manipulate it in some way. Students must not only demonstrate a grasp of the material, they must elaborate on what they have learned, make inferences beyond what is given in the text or during formal instruction, build adequate representations of key ideas and concepts, analyze and construct relationships, and make and defend nuanced judgments.

Thinking skills are particularly hard to measure. Crafting questions that will show the *result* of thinking is one thing, but getting a look at the *process* of thinking itself can be a challenge. Rigorous assessments are designed to make students' thinking more observable by giving students the opportunity to demonstrate their thinking process. In math class, for example, you might plan an end-of-unit, multiple-choice test that requires students to select the correct answer and explain why it is correct. Or if you're teaching a science unit on habitats, instead of ending the unit with a summative test that asks students to identify certain types of habitats and write a brief essay addressing the importance of habitat in sustaining a species, you might provide a description of a fictional bird and ask students to design (or select from several choices) a habitat that would attract and sustain that kind of bird and then defend their reasoning. Note how both these examples go beyond determining whether students know the material to uncover how well students understand what they have learned.

I don't mean to suggest that tests and quizzes that focus on factual recall have no place in a rigorous classroom. These assessments are fine as informal assessments that tell you whether students have acquired a basic understanding of the material. However, rigorous summative assessments go beyond asking students to *reproduce* what they have learned and focus on students' ability to *think about* and *use* what they have learned.

Rigorous Assessments Reinforce Rigorous Learning Experiences

It happens all the time. Students spend weeks involved in a lively and engaging learning unit that requires them to think and interact in highly rigorous ways. Then comes the summative assessment—and it's a typical paper-and-pencil test that emphasizes factual recall. The message? The point of the unit was not *really* to help students learn new ways of thinking about and interacting with the material; the point was for students to remember and regurgitate a series of facts. Unfortunately, this is typical of most assessment practices. Our tests don't reflect the kind of rigor that we say we expect from our students.

But what if we used our assessments as a way to extend the rigorous thinking and engagement stressed throughout the unit? The summative test, rather than being the end point, would be another learning tool to move students further ahead in their understanding.

For example, suppose you have spent an entire social studies unit discussing how food is grown, packaged, and delivered to the grocery store. A traditional final assessment might ask students to reproduce a diagram of the food supply chain. A rigorous assessment might ask each student to (1) create a poster that traces a single, assigned food item (perhaps a pumpkin seed, a chicken egg, or an apple seed) from the farm all the way to market and (2) present this poster to the class. Students need to apply their general grasp of the food supply chain to a specific category of food and apply general research skills to obtain the information. Then, students collectively expand their knowledge by sharing their projects and learning from one other.

Rigorous Assessments Stress Applications to Unpredictable and Real-World Situations

One of my favorite cooking shows is *Iron Chef America*. Unlike most cooking programs, where the chef plans dishes ahead of time, the chefs on *Iron Chef America* come to the kitchen without knowing what they will be preparing on the air. At the beginning of the show, they learn the name of the ingredient that they'll be expected to build a five-course meal around. Then they have one hour to produce that meal. On other cooking shows, the chef needs to demonstrate a recipe. On *Iron Chef America*, the chef needs to know how to cook.

Rigorous assessment is a little like *Iron Chef America*. Sure, students need to know the material, but they also need to understand it well enough to be able to apply it to or adapt it in a novel situation. In typical testing situations, students need to demonstrate mastery of the content. With a rigorous assessment, students need to know how to think.

In a typical testing situation, students re-engage with material they have worked with during the unit. They may be asked to solve a set of math problems very similar to the problems they have completed for homework, or to write an extended response exactly like the one they wrote during a practice classroom assignment. The material, by design, is very close to the material students have worked with throughout the unit. Yes, we have all learned that springing surprises on students during the final test is unfair. And without properly preparing students to deal with surprises, it *would* be unfair. But in a rigorous classroom, students learn to deal with unpredictable situations and learn how to use what they have learned in novel ways. When it is time for the assessment, they *are* prepared.

Take, for example, a language arts or English unit on narrative tone. Students learn what tone is, how to identify tone, and how authors use tone to convey an attitude about their subject. Students receive a list of a few words that might be used to establish tone, and they practice reading paragraphs and identifying the author's tone by choosing from among the listed words. Most units would stop there. The summative test might ask students to define tone, and to read a few sentences and choose the correct tone from among four options on a multiple-choice test.

A rigorous classroom's study of narrative tone takes students further. They might learn how to read passages (many of which are chosen from real-world examples, such as newspaper articles and blog posts), identify the author's tone, and explain how the author's tone influences their perception of the author's subject. On the summative assessment, students might read a passage they have never seen before, identify the author's tone, and explain how the author's tone affects their attitude toward the topic. Then, they might write a paragraph in a specific tone, selected from a list of choices. In these examples, students are not simply regurgitating what they have learned about tone and demonstrating their knowledge in a tightly contained testing situation that exactly mirrors their learning experience. They are asked to take what they have learned about tone and apply it to a new and novel situation. They must demonstrate the ability to analyze the effect that an author's tone has on their understanding of and attitude toward the material, and use tone effectively in their own writing.

✓ CHECKPOINT SUMMARY

Rigorous Assessments DO . . .	Rigorous Assessments DO NOT . . .
Sustain and extend rigorous instruction	Mark the end of instruction
Ask students to apply what they learn to real-world and unpredictable situations	Ask students to apply what they have learned to formulaic and predictable situations
Ask students to solve interesting problems	Ask students to do nothing more than solve algorithmic problems
Ask students to apply what they have learned	Ask students to do nothing more than remember what they have learned
Ask students to answer the how and why	Ask students to answer only the who, what, and when

THINK ABOUT . . .

Which of the three criteria for rigorous assessments resonates the most with you and why? What challenges might you face in creating and preparing students for rigorous assessments?

YOUR TURN

Acquire: Take a look at an upcoming test you plan to give your students. Compare your test to the criteria in this section. How does it measure up? In what ways does your test meet the criteria for rigorous assessment? In what ways does it not?

Apply: For your next unit, design or choose an assessment that meets at least one of the criteria for rigorous assessment.

Assimilate: Using the criteria provided in this section, examine a test you typically use in one of your unit and adjust it to be more rigorous.

Adapt: Using the criteria provided in this section, take a stab at increasing the rigor of the assessments you plan to use in an upcoming unit: not just the summative test at the unit's end but all the assessment measures used during instruction (quizzes, homework assignments, projects, discussion activities, and so on).

Creating Rigorous Summative Assessments

So how do you go about creating a rigorous assessment?

TAKE IT STEP BY STEP

How to Create a Rigorous Summative Assessment

1. Think about the kind of thinking you want students to engage in.
2. Select a summative task or tasks that require students to demonstrate that kind of thinking.
3. Determine the assessment's mastery threshold.
4. Determine the grading method.

Step 1: Think About the Kind of Thinking You Want Students to Engage In

What is the point of your learning unit? What skills will students acquire? At the end of the unit, what will students have learned that they did not know at the beginning of the unit? How will they be able to think differently after engaging in the unit? By answering these questions, you will look beyond what students will know and be able to do by the end of the unit to what students will be able to understand and how students will be able to think.

Step 2: Select a Summative Task or Tasks That Require Students to Demonstrate That Kind of Thinking

Summative assessments don't have to be paper-and-pencil tests. You might opt instead to have students complete a project, such as a multimedia display or a scale model; engage in a capstone experience, such as developing a social-action ad campaign or writing a final paper; develop a portfolio that demonstrates mastery; or complete a performance, such as giving a speech or participating in a debate. Any task that helps you determine how well students have mastered the learning and thinking objectives of your unit can be a summative assessment.

One way to determine the summative assessment task is to go back to your essential question (if you have one) and look at how students might answer it. For example, if your unit's essential question is "How can we find themes across multiple texts?" then your summative assessment should ask students to find themes across multiple texts. There are all sorts of ways to do this. You might, for instance,

- Ask students to read three poems and then write an essay in which they first identify the theme and then explain how each author develops the theme in the text.

- Provide students with a theme and a group of texts—essays, poems, short stories—and ask students to imagine they are editing an issue of a literary magazine focused on that theme. They must first select which three texts best demonstrate the theme and then write an essay that defends their choices.

- Create an assessment that requires students to adapt what they have learned about theme by applying the same strategy to visual texts, such as political cartoons, advertisements, and works of art.

Note how all of these assessment options satisfy the three criteria for a rigorous assessment. Each asks students to answer the essential question in a highly rigorous way. Each sustains or extends students' rigorous engagement by providing a highly rigorous task for them to complete. And each asks students to apply what they have learned to real-world or novel situations.

Step 3: Determine the Assessment's Mastery Threshold

The point of your summative assessment is to see whether students have mastered rigorous learning standards. Thus, you must determine the baseline level of performance you will accept as mastery. Most of us tend to think of mastery as the top level of understanding. But mastery, in most cases, is a *range* of performance characterized by a solid working knowledge of the targeted content and skills. It is important that you identify both the ceiling (the top level of possible performance for a given assessment) *and* the threshold (the baseline at which all students must competently perform). Any student who reaches this baseline has demonstrated mastery of the material. Any student who falls below it has not reached mastery and will need additional support. (For more on how to support students who do not reach mastery, see the *How to Support Struggling Students* guide in this series.)

Step 4: Determine the Grading Method

How will you grade your summative assessment? How will you provide students with feedback that tells them how well they have mastered the material and skills your assessment measures? Answering these questions before instruction helps you plan and develop a feedback loop that is consistent with how students will ultimately be assessed. Look beyond standard "points systems" to consider ways that will help students understand what they need to do to improve their performance on future assessments. In addition to traditional "total points" grades, you might use one of the following options:

- *Rubrics:* Rubrics make the learning objectives for the summative assessment explicit and highlight the criteria of mastery. Share the rubric with students ahead of time and prompt them to examine returned summative assessments with a copy of the rubric in hand, as it will provide clear feedback on how well they met the criteria.

- *Split points tied to the learning objectives:* Instead of giving students a single point total, calculate and present point totals for each learning objective in the unit. Thus, if your summative assessment has 30 questions (10 dealing with the unit's first objective, 5 with the second objective, and 15 with the third), students would receive 3 scores—a score for each learning objective. The total of the three scores would translate into the total grade, but students could also see how well they did on each learning objective.

Now it's time for you to try your hand at this approach by completing the **Rigorous Summative Assessment Planning Worksheet** on pages 33–34.

Assessment Formats to Consider

Let's look now at the practical question of what your rigorous summative assessment might look like. There are a number of formats that lend themselves to rigorous assessment.

"Best Answer" Multiple-Choice Tests

Although multiple-choice tests are often associated with soul-killing, drill-and-kill, downright boring instruction, they can be used in highly rigorous ways to assess how well students understand a concept. The difference between a typical multiple-choice test and a rigorous multiple-choice test is that in a typical test, there is only one right answer among the choices. In a rigorous multiple-choice test, students must select the best answer among several answer options that are "technically" or "almost" right.

Rigorous multiple-choice tests ask students to make nuanced judgments and to work their way through ambiguity.

Persuasive Writing Assignments

Persuasive writing assignments require students to analyze an issue, take a position, and defend it. The key is that students have to know more than just the facts about an issue; they have to make judgments about those facts, organize them in a persuasive way, and use those facts to make their case. Students might, for example, construct an argument as to why a British account of the start of the American Revolution is more plausible than an American account, or why scatter plots are a better way to represent data about students' grade performance on the last class quiz than bar graphs are.

Rigorous Summative Assessment Planning Worksheet

Unit Title

Unit Standard(s)/Objective(s)

Step 1: Think About the Kind of Thinking You Want Student to Engage In	
What kind of thinking is implied by the standard(s)/objective(s)?	
What key concepts should students understand by the end of this unit?	
How should students be able to use these concepts?	

(continued)

Rigorous Summative Assessment Planning Worksheet (cont.)

Step 2: Select Tasks That Require the Demonstration of That Kind of Thinking	
What will students who have mastered these concepts be able to do?	
What learning tasks will best help students demonstrate mastery of these concepts?	
Step 3: Determine the Assessment's Mastery Threshold	
What does mastery of the identified learning tasks look like?	
What is the mastery threshold?	
Step 4: Determine the Grading Method	
What feedback methods will tell students if they have reached the mastery threshold and how they can continue to improve?	

Persuasive writing goes beyond assessing whether students know the information to reveal how well they have thought the information through, can use it to generate new knowledge, and can organize the information for a particular purpose (in this case, to persuade).

INVENTION TASKS

Once students have learned a concept and identified the patterns, principles, and key elements of that concept, an invention task asks them to take what they have learned and create something of their own. For example, students might use the conceits of a Shakespearean sonnet to write their own, follow the principles of force and motion to design ways of protecting an egg dropped from the top of the school building, or apply what they've learned about nutrition to create their own diet plans.

Asking students to use what they have learned to invent something new not only tests their understanding of the concepts involved but also assesses their ability to apply and adapt these concepts to solve problems.

DECISION MAKING

An assessment built around decision making measures students' ability to analyze several options and come to a conclusion based on a defined set of criteria. It is a great way to test whether students can evaluate and choose among competing options, especially when there is no clear choice. Thus, you might end a unit by asking students to examine several stories they have read throughout the unit, determine which one is the best example of a fable, and defend their choice. You might ask them to tell you which of the Greek gods was the most heroic and why, or to explain which environment—water, moist cotton, or soil—is best for sprouting peas.

The combined task of deciding and explaining that decision not only tells you if students understand and can apply criteria but also reveals whether they can weigh several options and go on to make reasoned judgments through the application of appropriate criteria.

EXPLAIN YOUR ANSWERS

Lots of curriculum standards involve mastery of processes or computational tasks. One way to assess whether students understand what they are doing is to ask them to complete the task and then explain their answers or their process. For instance, you might have students explain or justify their answers to math problems using "non-calculator" reasons. Or you might have them complete a process, such as balancing a chemical equation, and then write a paragraph explaining why they took the steps they did or made the choices they made.

Asking students to explain their process helps you see not only if students correctly engaged in the process but whether they understood what they did and the reasons they did it.

ERROR ANALYSIS

In an error analysis assessment, students are given problems and answers. Some of the answers are correct and some are incorrect. Students must identify each answer as correct or incorrect and then explain why. For example, after a unit on compound sentences, you might give students a set of 10 sentences, 4 of which are properly constructed compound sentences and 6 of which are not. Students must then identify which of the 10 are compound sentences and transform the ones that are not into properly constructed compound sentences. Or you might ask students read the descriptions of seven living specimens, with each description listing the specimen's kingdom, phylum, order, class, family, and genus. Students must determine whether the classification is correct and explain why. And if the classification is not correct, they must explain where the errors are, why they are errors, and what the specimen's proper classification is.

Error analysis asks students to do more than reproduce the correct answer, and it helps you assess whether students understand why an answer is correct and whether students can create a correct answer from an incorrect one.

LEARNING PORTFOLIOS

This assessment approach allows students to track their own progress over time and analyze their growth in a particular area. Portfolio assessment invites students to evaluate their own learning and work with you to track their own growth. To create learning portfolios, start by setting final criteria for mastery for the unit of study. Then ask students to select examples of their work throughout the unit and write an essay in which they explain how the examples they chose demonstrate (1) how their understanding of the unit concepts has grown and (2) their development of the target skills. Students identify early learning challenges and how they overcame them, and they explain where they are now in terms of their own understanding. Finally, students use the artifacts they selected and the unit criteria to suggest and justify the grade they deserve. For example, students might spend an entire unit learning how to find the derivative. At the end of the unit, they would select exemplar homework assignments, quizzes, notes, and worksheets that demonstrate their progress in understanding derivatives over the course of the unit and then explain how they have come to understand how to find derivatives over time. Finally, students would make a case for their final grade, pointing to evidence from their work that they have met the learning criteria for the unit.

Portfolios are a great way for you and your students to use multiple artifacts to assess their mastery of the material or skills.

CAPSTONE EXPERIENCES

This project-based assessment format involves students taking all that they have learned in a unit (or even across multiple units) and synthesizing it. For example, students might spend a unit studying various family structures. At the end of the unit, they would create their own family tree and explain how their family fits into one or more of the structures they have studied. At the conclusion of a unit focused on various threats to the environment, students might identify what they believe to be the biggest threat, create a multimedia experience to inform the public of this environmental threat, and design a follow-up ad campaign to motivate the public to take action or change their behaviors. Or maybe students have just completed a poetry unit and will now work in groups to create their own anthology of poetry, selecting poems that contain an array of poetic devices and represent an array of styles. As a group, they would write the foreword to the anthology in which they explain why they selected the poems and also write introductions to each poem, pointing out key features and explaining how that poem supports the anthology's overall theme.

Capstone experiences are a great way to help students answer the "So what?" of a unit. They involve students reflecting on why they have learned what they have learned, and how the different parts of the unit connect in a meaningful way.

THINK ABOUT . . .

How might the choice of an assessment format affect the way that you plan the rest of a unit?

YOUR TURN

Acquire: Take a look at each assessment format in this section and make a list of the pros and cons of each. Which assessment formats lend themselves more to measurement of content mastery, and which formats seem better for assessing process or skill mastery? Which formats seem most suited to your grade level or course? Why?

Apply: Select one of the assessment formats to use for an upcoming unit test. Make your selection, and proceed through all four steps of planning a rigorous summative assessment.

Assimilate: Take a summative unit assessment you currently use and make it more rigorous by incorporating some of the features of the assessment formats discussed. For instance, if your test asks students to compute answers, add a question that requires students to explain their answers. If your test is multiple choice, change some of the distracters from "wrong" answers to "almost right answers" so that students must make nuanced judgments.

Adapt: Determine which components of your formative assessment plans naturally lead to one or more of the summative assessment formats discussed. Then map out the formative assessment strategies you will use to prepare students for the summative assessment format you have selected.

YES, BUT . . .

What about formative assessment?

Once you have determined how you will assess students' overall mastery of the learning goals and have created your summative assessment, then you can determine what formative assessment tools and strategies you will use to track students' progress toward those goals throughout your unit activities. Formative assessment helps you make sure that students are on track to mastery, and it can show you where you must intervene in order to keep them on pace and headed in the right direction. The data it provides can guide decisions about how to provide effective, proactive, and progressive support both before and during instruction to minimize destructive struggle and keep students on the path to mastery. (For more on how to use formative assessments to inform support for students, see the *How to Support Struggling Students* guide in this series.)

Any of the assessment formats covered in this section can be used in a formative way. Go ahead and apply the same criteria that you would use for summative assessment, but remember what you are measuring in formative assessment is *progress*, not mastery.

2

Selecting Rigorous
Learning Material

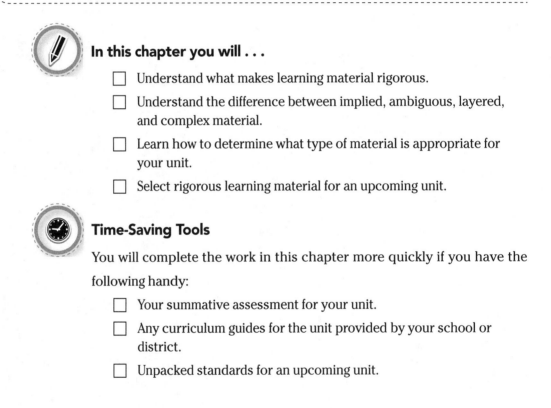

In this chapter you will . . .

- [ ] Understand what makes learning material rigorous.
- [ ] Understand the difference between implied, ambiguous, layered, and complex material.
- [ ] Learn how to determine what type of material is appropriate for your unit.
- [ ] Select rigorous learning material for an upcoming unit.

Time-Saving Tools

You will complete the work in this chapter more quickly if you have the following handy:

- [ ] Your summative assessment for your unit.
- [ ] Any curriculum guides for the unit provided by your school or district.
- [ ] Unpacked standards for an upcoming unit.

Once you have created a rigorous summative assessment for a unit, what content will foster the kind of thinking and learning necessary for mastery? The next step is to identify the rigorous learning material that will be the basis for your instruction.

Teachers don't always get to choose their content. We are often told what texts we will use, what worksheets we can provide, what supplemental material we can access, what kinds of assignments we can give, and what projects we can assign. But when you do have the choice, how can you ensure that you select highly rigorous learning material that promotes rigorous thinking?

In this chapter, we'll look at a comparison framework that will help you identify what makes some material more rigorous than other material. I'll show you how to make intelligent choices among various learning material options, based on your goals and your students' capacity for rigor. And if you do not have a choice in the material that will be the basis for your lessons, I'll show you how to find the most rigorous elements of the prescribed material so that you can emphasize them in instruction.

What Makes Learning Material Rigorous?

Rigorous learning material requires students to be active, not passive. It requires perseverance and discipline, as it asks students to use critical and creative thinking skills and background knowledge to impose meaning and reach understanding. As my colleague Kenyatta Graves explained to me recently, "When teachers have choices between one or another set of materials to use, materials that require students to reach for skills and concepts are more rigorous than those that place those same skills and concepts in a student's hands" (personal communication, 2010). In other words, the rigor of learning material is relative, and the kind of learning material to look for is that which is just within but at the outer edge of students' current abilities. Working with the material should require students to stretch—to employ critical and creative thinking and their background knowledge to construct new meaning and acquire new skills.

Typically material that is rigorous will have at least one of the following four characteristics: *implicit meaning*, *ambiguity*, *layers*, or *complexity*. Let's take a look at each.

Implicit Meaning

When material has *implicit meaning*—meaning that is not openly stated—students must work to uncover that meaning by logically considering context and supporting information. In a sense, they are required to complete an intellectual task that the content has begun, identifying relevant concepts, analyzing or synthesizing those concepts, and evaluating the concepts to reach a logical conclusion.

Learning material has implicit meaning when it

- Leaves some important ideas or key understandings unstated.
- Incorporates allusions, foreshadowing, or symbolism.
- Presents evidence within concepts but does not state a conclusion about the concepts' meaning or importance.
- Requires students to engage in logical interpretation and analysis.
- Restricts innumerable interpretations when the evidence is considered logically.

Learning material with implicit meaning is useful for helping students learn how to

- Construct understanding from context.
- Extrapolate key ideas that are unstated.
- Fill in gaps and bring background knowledge to bear on the current learning challenge.
- Synthesize several clues to determine the correct answer.
- Use evidence to detect and defend meaning.
- Use logic and reasoning skills to construct and extend meaning.
- Distinguish relevant information from irrelevant information.
- Interpret symbols, metaphors, and analogies.

Ambiguity

Unlike learning material with implicit meaning, where there is a single understanding that students must work to uncover, learning material with *ambiguity* is open-ended and susceptible to multiple interpretations. Because there isn't one "right" answer but many, students must decide what they think, take a stand, and defend it.

Ambiguity is good, but you want to avoid vagueness. If material is vague, its meaning is unclear. In ambiguous material, *several* possible meanings are clear, and students must choose the meaning that makes the best sense to them after weighing the relative value of each possible interpretation.

Learning material has ambiguity if it

- Contains symbols or images with multiple meanings.
- Contains nuance and subtlety.
- Contains several interpretations depending on the context.
- Requires the student to draw on prior knowledge or personal experiences for interpretation.
- Invites the student to analyze and evaluate interpretations offered by teachers and peers as equally valid or available.

Ambiguous learning material is useful for helping students learn how to

- Grapple with uncertainty or the abstract.
- Marshal evidence to defend a point of view.

- Choose and defend a position.
- Distinguish between and among points of view.
- Examine the point of view of others.
- Consider several alternatives.
- Evaluate evidence and ideas.
- Juggle multiple perspectives.
- Compare and contrast.
- Pick up on nuance and subtlety.
- Move beyond black-and-white thinking and learn to deal with shades of gray.
- Build interpretations.

Layers

Learning material that is *layered* requires students to use two or more successive cognitive functions in order to understand it. Because layered material contains multiple parts that are sequentially related, if the whole is to make sense, students must pursue understanding in a particular order. For example, students must analyze information before they evaluate it, or they must understand how a process works before they can apply it. To quote my colleague Kenyatta Graves again, "Layered material ensures that students understand intellectual methodologies. Meaning is only available when multiple skills or concepts are accessed in an ordered pattern particular to an academic discipline. Students construct their own meaning by handling academic tasks in a sequence that, if ignored, reveals inaccuracies or incomplete conclusions" (personal communication, 2010).

Rather than offer a surface understanding of a concept, layered learning material asks students to look into successively deeper aspects of the concept in question. The more students dig, the more they understand.

Learning material is layered when it

- Asks students to build their understanding through systematic inquiry.
- Contains multiple steps that must be pursued in a particular order.
- Contains tasks that grow in cognitive demand.
- Contains sequential ordering of multiple data sources, elements, evidence, or variables.

Layered material helps students to

- Understand intellectual methodologies.
- Monitor their own learning.
- Access increasingly more demanding material and skills.
- Engage in systematic inquiry and dig for meaning.
- Develop deductive or inductive reasoning skills.
- Build on previously learned knowledge and skills.
- Follow a logical order to reach a conclusion.
- Follow a train of thought to its logical conclusion.
- Think systematically.
- Combine successive cognitive tasks in order to solve problems.

Complexity

Whereas learning material with layers contains multiple but sequential steps, learning material with *complexity* contains multiple parts that may or may not require a sequential order. Complex material contains "multiple solutions, and the total path is not visible from any single vantage point" (Byrnes, 1996, p. 73).

Learning material is complex when it asks students to consider a number of variables or data points, a series of overlapping ideas, or several interrelated concepts. There may be different kind of relationships between and among the various elements. The task for students is to detect patterns and understand these relationships; it's this quest for understanding that makes complex learning material rigorous and differentiates it from material we might describe as "complicated" (that is, simply composed of multiple parts or elements). When material is complex, its meaning is not obvious to students and won't become obvious until students detect the patterns inherent within the interrelated concepts and relationships, some of which change based on context.

Material is complex when it has

- Multiple components, concepts, data sources, or other elements.
- Multiple relationships among various elements, which may or may not be consistent.
- Multiple pathways that lead to understanding or a solution.
- Nonlinear relationships among the variables.

Complex material helps students learn how to

- Manage multiple variables.
- Detect relationships among and between variables.
- Impose order on seeming disorder.
- Construct meaning by engaging in disciplined inquiry under conditions of uncertainty.
- Organize and rearrange knowledge in light of new information.
- Generate hypotheses.
- Represent knowledge in a variety of ways.
- Classify information.
- Compare and contrast.

CHECKPOINT SUMMARY

Implicit Meaning	Ambiguity	Layers	Complexity
Single meaning	Multiple meanings	Sequential relationships	Multiple relationships
Relies on context	Relies on interpretation	Relies on ordered patterns	Relies on relationships
Great for teaching abstracting and deduction	Great for teaching evaluation, induction, and error analysis (interpretation)	Great for teaching cause/effect and error analysis (process)	Great for teaching compare/contrast, induction, and classification

Selecting Rigorous Learning Material

The first step in selecting rigorous learning material is to examine your unit's summative assessment. What kind of thinking does your assessment emphasize? What learning goals does your assessment measure? Answer these questions and then consider: What type of learning material will best help students engage in that kind of thinking and reach each goal?

For instance, if one of your goals is to help students understand the relationships among the national economies of various countries, you might consider *complex material* that will give students opportunities to work with multiple variables and relationships. However, if your learning goal is to help students determine which economic structure is best suited for a primarily agrarian culture, then *ambiguous material* would likely give students a better chance to evaluate variables and make a determination.

Of course, a typical unit has multiple learning goals, addressed through multiple lessons. Each goal is best pursued through different thinking processes and, thus, with material characterized by different aspects and degrees of rigor.

When selecting learning material for a unit, I recommend following a basic decision-making process focused on first considering the *kinds of thinking* associated with mastery of each learning goal and then analyzing the degree to which the learning materials you are considering reflect the characteristics of the four types of rigor. Begin by completing the **Learning Goal Rigor-Analysis Worksheet** (see page 48), which is designed to help clarify the kind of thinking and thinking processes students need in order to master the goal in question. Next, fill in a copy of the **Learning Material Rigor-Analysis Worksheet** (see page 49) for all learning material under consideration, checking off the characteristics that apply and making notes to yourself that capture specific examples, if you desire. Finally, use the data you captured in these worksheets to complete the **Learning Material Decision-Making Template** (see page 51). This matrix asks you to translate your analyses into numerical ratings associated with each type of rigor. Once you've filled in your ratings, determining the best choice of rigorous learning material becomes a simple matter of multiplication.

Learning Goal Rigor-Analysis Worksheet

Learning Goal:			
To master this learning goal, it is important that students learn how to			
☐ Construct understanding from context ☐ Extrapolate key ideas that are unstated ☐ Fill in gaps and bring background knowledge to bear on the current learning challenge ☐ Synthesize several clues to determine the correct answer ☐ Use evidence to detect and defend meaning ☐ Use logic and reasoning skills to construct and extend meaning ☐ Distinguish relevant information from irrelevant information ☐ Interpret symbols, metaphors, and analogies	☐ Grapple with uncertainty or the abstract ☐ Choose and defend a position ☐ Distinguish between and among points of view ☐ Examine another's point of view ☐ Consider several alternatives ☐ Evaluate evidence and ideas ☐ Juggle multiple perspectives ☐ Compare and contrast ☐ Pick up on nuance and subtlety ☐ Move beyond black-and-white thinking and learn to deal with shades of gray ☐ Build interpretations	☐ Understand intellectual methodologies ☐ Monitor their own learning ☐ Access increasingly more demanding material and/or skills ☐ Engage in systematic inquiry and dig for meaning by peeling back successive layers ☐ Develop deductive or inductive reasoning skills ☐ Follow a logical order to reach a conclusion ☐ Follow a train of thought to its logical conclusion ☐ Think systematically ☐ Combine successive cognitive tasks in order to solve problems	☐ Manage multiple variables ☐ Detect relationships among and between variables ☐ Impose order on seeming disorder ☐ Construct meaning by engaging in discipline inquiry under conditions of uncertainty ☐ Organize and rearrange knowledge in light of new information ☐ Generate hypotheses ☐ Represent knowledge in a variety of ways ☐ Classify information ☐ Compare and contrast
Seek Material with Implicit Meaning	**Seek Material with Ambiguity**	**Seek Material with Layers**	**Seek Material with Complexity**

Learning Material Rigor-Analysis Worksheet

Learning Material:			
This learning material has the following characteristics:			
☐ Leaves some important ideas unstated ☐ Incorporates allusions, foreshadowing, or symbolism ☐ Presents evidence within concepts but does not state a conclusion ☐ Requires students to engage in logical interpretation and analysis ☐ Restricts innumerable interpretations when the evidence is considered logically	☐ Contains symbols or images with multiple meanings ☐ Contains nuance and subtlety ☐ Contains several interpretations depending on the context ☐ Requires the student to draw on prior knowledge or personal experiences for interpretation ☐ Invites the student to analyze and evaluate interpretations offered by teachers and peers as equally valid or available	☐ Asks students to build their understanding through systematic inquiry ☐ Contains multiple steps which must be pursued in a particular order ☐ Contains tasks that grow in cognitive demand ☐ Contains sequential ordering of multiple data sources, elements, evidence, or variables	☐ Features multiple components, concepts, data sources, or other elements ☐ Features multiple relationships among various elements, which may or may not be consistent ☐ Contains multiple pathways toward understanding or solving a problem ☐ Features nonlinear relationships among the variables
Implicit Meaning	**Ambiguity**	**Layers**	**Complexity**

To Complete the Learning Material Decision-Making Template

1. Identify and fill in the target learning goal that will be included on the unit's summative assessment.

2. Look at your completed **Learning Goal Rigor-Analysis Worksheet** and consider the number of checkmarks in each column (corresponding to the different criteria of rigor). Then, for each of the four criteria of rigor, choose the rating that best applies:

> This criterion of rigor is
>
> 3 = critically important to the mastery of this learning goal.
>
> 2 = important but not critical to mastery.
>
> 1 = not very important to mastery.
>
> 0 = unrelated to mastery.

Write your rating in the blank space next to each of the criteria in the "Criteria Value" portion of the matrix, then copy that number across the entire row, putting it in the first blank in every column in the "Learning Material Options Under Consideration" portion of the matrix.

3. Staying in the "Learning Material Options Under Consideration" portion of the matrix, enter a brief description of the various materials you are considering using in your focus on this learning goal. Next look the data you captured in each **Learning Material Rigor-Analysis Worksheet** you completed, decide the degree to which each of the options possesses *implicit meaning, ambiguity, layers,* and *complexity.* Use this scale:

> This learning material
>
> 3 = reflects the characteristics of this type of rigor to a very significant degree.
>
> 2 = reflects the characteristics of this type of rigor to some degree, but not completely.
>
> 1 = reflects the characteristics of this type of rigor only a little bit.
>
> 0 = is not characteristics of this type of rigor.

Write your rating in the second blank of the column devoted to that option.

4. Multiply the two numbers in each cell to find the column total for all of the learning material options.

5. Add the totals in each column to calculate each option's final score.

The item with the highest score represents the best choice of rigorous learning material. In the case of a tie, choose the item that you like the most or that is most relevant to students' lives.

Learning Material Decision-Making Template

Unit Title				
Learning Goal				
Criteria Value	**Learning Material Options Under Consideration**			
For the pursuit of this learning goal, how important is it for the material to have . . .	*To what degree does each exhibit the criteria of rigorous learning material?*			
Implicit Meaning: _____	___ × ___	___ × ___	___ × ___	___ × ___
Ambiguity: _____	___ × ___	___ × ___	___ × ___	___ × ___
Layers: _____	___ × ___	___ × ___	___ × ___	___ × ___
Complexity: _____	___ × ___	___ × ___	___ × ___	___ × ___
Total				

LANGUAGE ARTS EXAMPLE

Suppose you are helping students learn how to understand plot development in a short story. Your learning goal for this lesson is to help students see how one plot element leads to the next, but you don't want to confuse them by giving them a story that does not follow prototypical plot development.

You have a choice among four short stories. Story A contains a very sequential plot structure with some symbolism and implicit meaning. Story B has a sequential plot structure, but the plot structure is pretty simplistic. It also has minimal symbolism and implicit meaning but a complex set of characters that may confuse students. Story C has no symbolism or implicit meaning. It does contain several plot elements that build to a straightforward conclusion, but it has so many characters that the students may have difficulty following the plot. Story D has some implicit meaning and a sequential plot that helps students see how plot elements build in a story, but the story does contain some complexity that may confuse struggling learners, and it has minimal ambiguity. Here is how you might complete the Learning Material Decision-Making Template:

Learning Goal: Students will understand how plot elements work together to bring a story to its conclusion.					
Criteria Value		**Learning Material Options Under Consideration**			
For the pursuit of this learning goal, how important is it for the material to have . . .		*To what degree does each exhibit the criteria of rigorous learning material?*			
		Story A	**Story B**	**Story C**	**Story D**
Implicit Meaning:	1	$1 \times 2 = 2$	$1 \times 1 = 1$	$1 \times 0 = 0$	$1 \times 2 = 2$
Ambiguity:	1	$1 \times 2 = 2$	$1 \times 1 = 1$	$1 \times 0 = 0$	$1 \times 1 = 1$
Layers:	3	$3 \times 3 = 9$	$3 \times 2 = 6$	$3 \times 3 = 9$	$3 \times 3 = 9$
Complexity:	0	$0 \times 0 = 0$	$0 \times 3 = 0$	$0 \times 3 = 0$	$0 \times 1 = 0$
Total		13	8	9	12

Here, Story A will be the best choice. But because the score for Story A and Story D are so close, you might choose Story D if you think that the higher degree of ambiguity in Story A may detract from students' ability to detect plot structure.

MATH EXAMPLE

Imagine you want to help your students practice solving for x using the distributive property. Based on your goal, you decide that you need to help students manage both layered and complex material in order to help them learn how to develop a sequential way of grappling with multiple variables. You don't want to confuse students by introducing ambiguity or implicit meaning (you want students to focus on developing ordered ways of solving problems without getting bogged down in trying to uncover unstated meaning or juggling multiple meanings). You are considering between three different types of materials: (1) problems from the math textbook, (2) a group project in which students solve a set of problems in order to solve a mystery, or (3) a math learning video game in which students practice solving problems in order to fight off world domination by space aliens. Here's how you might complete the matrix:

Learning Goal: Students will learn how to solve for x using the distributive property.

Criteria Value		Learning Options Under Consideration		
For the pursuit of this learning goal, how important is it for the material to have . . .		*To what degree does each possess the criteria of rigorous learning material?*		
		Problems from the textbook	**Math Mystery group project**	**Math learning video game**
Implicit Meaning:	1	$1 \times 0 = 0$	$1 \times 2 = 2$	$1 \times 3 = 3$
Ambiguity:	1	$1 \times 0 = 0$	$1 \times 3 = 3$	$1 \times 1 = 1$
Layers:	3	$3 \times 3 = 9$	$3 \times 2 = 6$	$3 \times 3 = 9$
Complexity:	3	$3 \times 3 = 9$	$3 \times 3 = 9$	$3 \times 3 = 9$
Total		18	20	22

In this case, the math learning video game is the best choice of rigorous learning material.

Other Selection Considerations

When selecting rigorous learning material, there are several other tips to consider, any of which might serve as a tiebreaker when you're torn between options.

- *Make sure that learning material is grade- and age-appropriate.* Remember, just because learning material is rigorous according to the guidelines in this chapter does not mean that it is age- or grade-appropriate for the students you teach. Sometimes material requires reading skills that are outside students' reach or deals with subjects that are too mature for them.

- *Try to select learning material that is relevant and relatable.* Learning material that is directly related to students' lives is far superior to material that is unrelated and contrived. When you can, opt for material that has real-world implications; it provides greater context for learning and invites greater student interest and involvement.

- ***Build students' capacity to engage with rigorous learning material over time.*** Students' capacity to grapple with rigorous material develops gradually. As a rule of thumb, move from material with implicit meaning (containing one unstated meaning) to material that is ambiguous (containing multiple meanings), and from material with layers (focuses on one process with multiple steps) to material that is complex (incorporating multiple processes with multiple interrelated steps). If you are unsure which learning material to choose, start with some that has implicit meaning and layers, moving on to ambiguous and complex material as students' ability to successfully grapple with rigorous material grows over time.

- ***Make sure learning material is directly connected to your learning goals.*** While learning material may be rigorous, if it does not help students achieve your learning goals, it doesn't serve you or your students well. When you have the choice between (1) material that is rigorous but only tangentially related to your learning goals and (2) material that is less rigorous but more directly related to your learning goals, *choose the learning material that most closely aligns with your goals.* Even though it may not be as rigorous, you can select a learning experience that will help students engage with that material in a highly rigorous way. (See Chapter 3.)

- ***Choose learning material that most matches the content students will face on the summative assessment.*** It is important to give students practice with the same type of material they will face on the summative assessment. In this way, they develop proficiency working with this type of material, and you can be sure that the material you select is as rigorous as the material on the test will be.

THINK ABOUT . . .

How does the selection of learning material drive the instructional choices you will make? What should come first, the selection of learning material or the selection of instructional strategies? Why?

YOUR TURN

Acquire: Gather together all the learning material you plan to use in an upcoming unit and analyze it for rigor, identifying implicit meaning, ambiguity, layers, and complexity.

Apply: Think about the next unit you plan to teach and how you might incorporate learning material with greater degrees of rigor. Identify where students would benefit from material that contains greater degrees of implicit meaning, ambiguity, layers, or complexity.

Assimilate: Look at your next unit. How might you make it more rigorous? Look for opportunities to add rigorous learning material or replace existing material with learning material that is more rigorous.

Adapt: Consider how you might adjust the learning material in an upcoming unit to differentiate it for students. How might you increase rigor for students who are ready for more challenge? What strategies could you use to help struggling students access the rigorous learning material you've chosen?

YES, BUT . . .

What if I don't have choices about the learning material I use?

You can still unearth the rigorous elements of the material you have. For instance, if your students must read a particular novel or have to use a particular basal reader or anthology, you can still emphasize those parts of the material that have implicit meaning, ambiguity, layers, and complexity. Perhaps you are required to use a certain textbook or to cover material that doesn't seem particularly rigorous; you can supplement it with additional readings to give students more rigorous information on the topic.

When you don't have a choice about the material you use, or you want to increase the rigor of existing material, there are a couple of strategies to try.

Put learning material in conversation with other material. Instead of using a single source or activity, pair material in ways that create ambiguity, complexity, or layers. For example, rather than simply have your students read the one account of the French and Indian War in the textbook, provide additional readings such as an account from the French perspective and an account from the British one. This introduces ambiguity to seemingly unambiguous material. To introduce complexity, give students several primary documents to read or several variables in an experiment and ask them to detect patterns. You can increase the layers in material by, for example, giving students math problems in which they must solve several smaller problems in order to arrive at the solution to the primary problem.

Selectively withhold information. Sometimes you can increase the rigor of learning material by omitting some information and requiring students to fill it in themselves. Be careful here. Withholding essential facts or steps is just cruel. However, withholding information while leaving critical clues can help students learn how to create meaning from context and by using logic—the way you might go about solving a good Sudoku puzzle. For instance, you might give students paragraphs with key words missing in order to teach them how to use context clues to figure out the meaning or how to identify sentence structure. You might give students word problems with key information missing and then ask them to tell you what information they need; this can help them learn the key elements of a particular type of math problem. Or you might give students a science experiment that is partially completed and ask them to use what they know of the scientific method to fill in the rest.

No matter what curriculum you're working from, you can always highlight the parts that are more rigorous and plan learning experiences with the material that will help students engage with it in a highly rigorous way. The next chapter will show you how to do just that.

Choosing Rigorous
Instructional Strategies

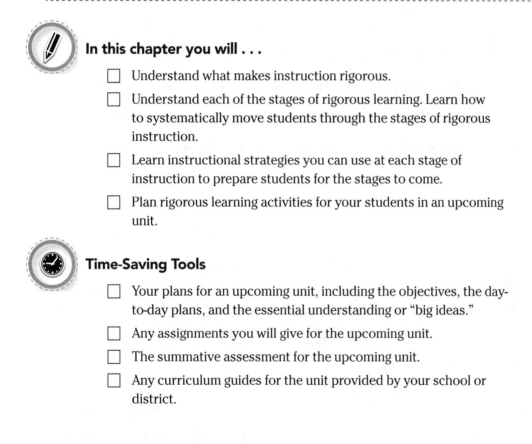

In this chapter you will . . .

- [ ] Understand what makes instruction rigorous.
- [ ] Understand each of the stages of rigorous learning. Learn how to systematically move students through the stages of rigorous instruction.
- [ ] Learn instructional strategies you can use at each stage of instruction to prepare students for the stages to come.
- [ ] Plan rigorous learning activities for your students in an upcoming unit.

Time-Saving Tools

- [ ] Your plans for an upcoming unit, including the objectives, the day-to-day plans, and the essential understanding or "big ideas."
- [ ] Any assignments you will give for the upcoming unit.
- [ ] The summative assessment for the upcoming unit.
- [ ] Any curriculum guides for the unit provided by your school or district.

Now that you have your learning material set, which instructional strategies will you use to move students toward rigorous mastery of your standards and objectives? Your next task is to plan rigorous learning experiences.

Rigorous learning materials alone do not guarantee that a lesson will be rigorous. If students are asked to interact with rigorous material in a simplistic or rote manner or if the learning activities around that material do not ask them to make their own meaning and practice rigorous thinking and problem solving, the lesson will not be rigorous.

In this chapter, we will examine instructional strategies that will allow your students to interact with content in a rigorous manner. Rigorous instruction is the way to fulfill the promise of rigorous material and can even make up for the limitations of any less-than-rigorous materials you may be required to use.

What Makes Instruction Rigorous?

Rigorous instruction is characterized by learning experiences that help students make meaning for themselves. Rigorous instructional strategies are how teachers help students learn how to manipulate, reorganize, and adapt what they are learning to new situations and apply what they are learning to new and novel contexts. For example, if a student is asked to *compare* the presidency of George Washington to that of Abraham Lincoln, he will invariably learn something about both presidencies he hadn't learned before. His teacher could have had this student and his classmates memorize facts about both presidencies, but instead, she asks them to manipulate those facts in a way that helps students develop new ideas about both presidencies. And that's it in a nutshell: Rigorous instructional strategies promote the kind of thinking that goes beyond recalling information and performing procedures. It asks students to extend and refine their thinking and reach for greater understanding.

The Four Stages of Rigorous Instruction

We cannot expect students to just jump in and be able to start thinking in a highly rigorous way. But we *can* build students' capacity to engage in rigorous learning through the instructional choices we make. The International Center for Leadership in Education (2008) has developed a "Rigor/Relevance Framework" that separates rigorous learning into four distinct stages of instruction. I've used these stage names as the basis for my own definitions (which are, in some cases, very different from the originals):

1. *Acquisition*, where you focus on helping students understand new content and acquire new skills.

2. *Application*, where you focus on helping students apply thinking skills so that they can use what they are learning in a meaningful way.

3. *Assimilation*, where you focus on helping students use thinking processes to synthesize what they are learning into new understanding.

4. *Adaptation*, where you help students develop habits of mind and apply what they have learned to new contexts across disciplines.

Although it is convenient to examine rigorous instruction in these four stages, keep in mind that rigorous instruction is often integrated. While all four stages are necessary to build students' capacity to engage in rigorous thinking and learning, they are not necessarily linear. Often, you will help students work in more than one stage at a time, acquiring new information as they apply it, for instance, or assimilating information as they adapt it. Thus, while I may refer to "an acquisition lesson," keep in mind that you need not necessarily design a single lesson around a single stage. Sometimes you'll move from acquisition to application in the same lesson, which may span a portion of a class period, an entire class period, or several class periods.

By the way, it's no accident that the names of these stages of rigorous learning mirror the "Your Turn" stages in this series. In the same way that you develop, refine, and integrate your own teaching skills as you move toward mastery of the principles of great teaching, you should be helping your students rigorously develop their own capacity as *they* move toward mastery of the content and standards of your course or grade level.

Let's take a look now at each of the stages of rigorous instruction, examining the kinds of thinking and learning that happen at each stage as well as ways to support and facilitate that thinking and learning. You will have an opportunity to practice planning lessons that move students from one stage to the next. In **Appendix A**, you'll find further guidance on developmentally appropriate instructional practices for the students you teach and the kinds of rigorous materials you'll be using.

Acquisition

Key Question: How will you help your students understand content and acquire skills in a rigorous way?

At the acquisition stage of a unit, you are helping students store new information and learn new skills. Typical acquisition lessons ask students to simply memorize information; this is how some students come to know the multiplication tables without really understanding how to multiply, or are able to read a passage and decode words without really understanding the passage's main idea.

Unfortunately, many teachers do not see acquisition as a rigorous stage of learning. We try to help students quickly acquire new information and knowledge and "master the basics" so that they can *then* engage in rigorous thinking and learning. But acquisition lessons done correctly are rigorous all on their own. All learning units contain some form of acquisition, but the difference between rigorous and unrigorous acquisition is in how you ask students to organize what they have learned. When you design lessons that help students store information in short- and long-term memory, link new knowledge to prior knowledge, organize new information so that it is available and can be manipulated during lessons that focus on stages of rigor, you help students deepen their understanding of new concepts and skills by creating meaning for themselves.

The truth is, how we ask students to learn new information or skills not only can be rigorous in and of itself, but it can also prepare students for even higher levels of rigor.

GUIDELINES FOR RIGOROUS ACQUISITION LESSONS

Here are five things teachers can do to facilitate rigorous acquisition.

Help Students Organize New Learning for Future Application

The idea of rigorous acquisition lessons is to make it easier for students to use newly acquired information and skills in rigorous lessons later on. For instance, if you know that you will want students to use the facts that they are learning about various types of foods to evaluate those foods' nutritional value and then develop an ideal menu, having students organize those facts into broader categories (e.g., food group, living and nonliving, and nutritional value) as they are learning them will facilitate comparison and evaluation later in the unit.

Give Students a Reason to Learn the New Content

Clarifying for students why they need to know, for example, the dates for certain historical events or the formulas for certain equations helps them understand where to store that information in their long-term memories. It also helps students prioritize their learning and focus on the aspects of the content that will be most relevant to later learning tasks. If, for instance, your purpose in presenting a certain set of historical facts is to prepare students to trace the causes of the French and Indian War, you will want them to pay attention to different features of those events than you would if your purpose was to have them understand these events in terms of Native Americans' conflicts with colonists.

Help Students Compare New Learning to What They Already Know

The point here is to facilitate knowledge integration, which sets students up for more effective assimilation of concepts and skills down the line. So, for example, you might prompt students learning about the nervous system to compare what they are learning to what they already know about the circulatory system. Or you might direct students learning about scatter plots to compare what they are learning to what they already know about bell curves.

Present New Learning as Part of Broader Principles and Knowledge

Your ultimate goal is to help students acquire big ideas and understandings—the patterns and principles that link smaller "bites" of information together. So rather than teach students the separate pronunciations of *bit*, *sit*, *kit*, and *fit*, you want to teach them the principle of pronunciation for words that end in *-it*. Instead of just teaching students disconnected formulas for calculating area, you want to teach them the mathematical elements and principles that undergird area and why these are important.

Embed New Learning into the Other Stages of Rigorous Instruction

Instead of teaching basic skills first before allowing students to interact with material in rigorous ways, teach students new content in the midst of solving problems. For instance, you might teach students how to count by 2s, 5s, and 10s by giving them play money and letting them "buy" items in a school store (application). Or you might teach students about the different forms of government by challenging them to set up a classroom society (adaptation).

INSTRUCTIONAL STRATEGIES FOR ACQUISITION

The following teaching strategies can help students actively process new information and learn in a much more rigorous way.

Have Students Work in Collaborative Pairs

Collaborative pairwork gives students opportunities to reflect on what they are learning as they work with a partner and see the content from an alternative perspective. Research has shown that this type of interaction not only facilitates knowledge development but also creates an awareness and understanding of knowledge that is difficult to develop without such interaction (Marzano, 2007).

Use Graphic Organizers

Graphic organizers are a powerful way to help students see some of the ways that information can be organized and stored. Research indicates that having students complete graphic organizers as they learn facilitates their understanding of the connections among and between pieces of information, and positions them to more efficiently access and use the information as they move through the learning process (Hattie, 2009; Marzano, Pickering, & Pollock, 2001; Thompson & Thompson, 2009). For detailed instructions on how to use graphic organizers to facilitate and support learning, see *How to Support Struggling Students*, another guide in this series.

LEARN MORE Online

Sample Graphic Organizers

- Story Maps
- Word Maps
- Concept Maps
- Frayer Models
- Semantic Maps

- Matrixes
- Causation Graphic Organizer
- Comparison Maps
- Note-Taking Graphic Organizers

You can download examples of these graphic organizers at www.mindstepsinc.com/rigor.

Ask Students to Create Nonlinguistic Representations

The process of creating nonlinguistic representations supports students' information processing. Students access multiple parts of their brains as they take information and then create an image, diagram, model, mental picture, or other graphic representation. Research has shown that when students take verbal and written information and transform it into a picture, they deepen their understanding of the concept and are more likely to store the information in their long-term memory (Marzano, 2007; Marzano et al., 2001).

Ask Provocative Questions

The questions a teacher poses during rigorous instruction go beyond asking students to recall facts; they invite students to think about and react to what they are learning in a personal and emotional way. Research tells us that these kinds of questions help students remember and process information much more deeply than they would if they simply memorized facts and mechanically executed procedures (Strong, Silver, & Perini, 2001).

Ask Students to Summarize

Summarizing gives students a chance to take what they are learning, encapsulate their understanding, and translate it into their own terms. Summarizing has been shown to be one of the most powerful ways of helping students learn and retain information (Marzano, 2007). It not only helps students store information but also helps them begin to create meaning for themselves. During an acquisition lesson, students ought to have several regular opportunities to summarize—in collaborative pairs, in brief written form, or in summarizer activities, like exit tickets or the creation of a histogram that captures what they have learning. Doing so helps them retain and process what they are learning in a highly rigorous way.

Use Mnemonics or Other Memory Strategies

Giving students a mnemonic for remembering facts helps them recall those facts more easily; giving students a mnemonic for remembering steps in a process helps them complete those steps more efficiently. The goal here is to facilitate students' organization, storage, and recall of new learning. Mnemonic strategies are sometimes dismissed as "low-level" instruction, useful only for "rote learning," but research has shown that they that can in fact facilitate deeper understanding of information when employed to involve higher-order thinking processes (Marzano, 2007).

How to Structure an Acquisition Lesson

When helping students acquire knowledge and skills, it is important to plan learning experiences that help them retain new information, organize it, retrieve it, and understand it. You can do this by structuring the lessons according to the following outline:

1. ***Establish an acquisition objective.*** Determine what knowledge and skills you want students to acquire in your lesson or unit.

2. ***Prepare students for learning.*** It is important to set students up to learn successfully. You can accomplish this by activating prior knowledge and, if necessary, preteaching requisite learning skills. (For more information on how to do this, see the *How to Support Struggling Students* guide in this series.)

3. ***Provide direct instruction.*** Introduce the new content and skills to students, and explain what they are, why they are important, and how students can effectively learn and use them.

4. ***Provide guided practice.*** Guided practice gives students a chance to internalize new knowledge and skills. Provide several practice opportunities, pointing out potential pitfalls and common errors, showing students how to avoid and correct these, and demonstrating alternative ways of using the knowledge and skills students are learning.

5. ***Use ongoing assessment strategies to monitor students' progress.*** These assessments will provide feedback to you and to students so that they can adjust their understanding and performance before persistent misconceptions take hold and interfere with mastery.

Take a look at the **Sample Acquisition Lesson Plan** on page 66, which is part of a 7th grade science unit on temperature change and endothermic reactions. The standard is that *students will use data collection devices to measure the temperature change involved in an endothermic reaction.* But before students can get there, they must first understand how to graph temperatures on the Fahrenheit and Celsius scales and how to determine the conversion between the two temperature sets. These concepts require an acquisition lesson.

As you can see, the teacher begins by identifying the key content and skills students will need to eventually be able to meet the standard. Then the teacher provides a way to help students organize the differences between Fahrenheit and Celsius so that students can remember them much more easily. The teacher also uses a "share and compare" strategy to make sure that students take thorough notes and have time to process the notes they take. But what makes this lesson truly rigorous is that the teacher asks students to go beyond just converting temperature from one form of measurement to another, to understanding *how* that conversion process works.

Now turn your attention to the unit you focused on in Chapters 1 and 2. How might you help students acquire the content and processes associated with mastery of that unit's standard or standards? Use the **Acquisition Lesson Planning Worksheet** on p. 67 and map out a plan.

Sample Acquisition Lesson Plan

Acquisition Objectives		
• Students will be able to define these terms: Fahrenheit, Celsius, temperature, and measurement. • Students will be able to measure temperature in Fahrenheit. • Students will be able to measure temperature in Celsius. • Students will be able to convert Fahrenheit temperatures to Celsius and vice versa.		
Content	**Skills/Processes**	**Learning Materials**
• Fahrenheit • Celsius • Temperature • Measurement • The difference between Fahrenheit and Celsius	• Measuring temperature in Fahrenheit • Measuring temperature in Celsius • Converting Fahrenheit temperature to Celsius • Converting Celsius temperature to Fahrenheit	Note-taking graphic organizer, worksheet, textbook exercises (pp. 47–48) for homework, paragraph prompt
Instructional Strategies		
Direct Instruction: • Activator: *Why are there two measuring systems?* Intro to Content 1. Lecture on temperature, with students taking notes on a graphic organizer, then working in collaborative pairs to share, compare, and complete each other's notes Intro to Skills/Processes 2. Lecture/demonstration on how to convert Fahrenheit to Celsius and vice versa 3. Class discussion of differences between the same temperature reading in Celsius and Fahrenheit	*Guided Practice:* 1. Practice activity measuring temperature in Fahrenheit and Celsius 2. Worksheet and collaborative pairwork to practice converting temperature 3. In-class writing assignment: "What is the difference between 22 degrees Celsius and 22 degrees Fahrenheit?"	*Independent Practice:* 1. Homework on converting temperature
Ongoing Assessment Strategies and Plans for Formative Responses		
• Review of homework assignments and adjustment of class discussion topic plans, as needed • In-class writing assignment		

Acquisition Lesson Planning Worksheet

Acquisition Objective(s)		

Content	Skills/Processes	Learning Materials

Instructional Strategies		
Direct Instruction: • Activator: Intro to Content Intro to Skills/Processes	*Guided Practice:*	*Independent Practice:*

Ongoing Assessment Strategies and Plans for Formative Responses

THINK ABOUT . . .

What are some specific ways you might make the acquisition portion of your lessons more rigorous?

YOUR TURN

Acquire: Take a look back at the research-based instructional strategies for acquisition on pages 62–64. Select one or two that you'd like to learn more about, and try them with your students during an acquisition lesson in an upcoming unit.

Apply: Think about a unit you are planning to teach within the next two weeks. Create an acquisition lesson plan incorporating one or more of the instructional strategies listed on pages 62–64.

Assimilate: Think about how you help students acquire new information. Which of the instructional strategies listed on pages 62–64 do you use already? Which might you add to your repertoire in your next unit? Adjust an upcoming acquisition lesson plan to include a new strategy.

Adapt: Think about how you help students acquire new information. Select one or more of the instructional strategies you currently use for acquisition lessons and use the guidelines on pages 61–62 to make them more rigorous.

Application

Key Question: How will you help your students apply what they are learning in a meaningful way?

Whereas acquisition is primarily concerned with collecting, storing, and organizing new knowledge, the application stage of rigorous instruction focuses on helping students develop the thinking skills they need to process and use what they have learned in a meaningful way. So we might see students take the different types of animals they have just learned about and classify them according to whether the animal is predator or prey, or take what they have just learned about character development in a story and use it to compare and contrast the way two different authors develop characters in their short stories. Application also asks students to take definitions, formulas, principles, theorems, and so on learned during acquisition and use them to solve problems. For instance, a low-rigor application lesson might ask students to solve contrived and predictable problems such as "Use the formula $F = ma$ to complete the problems at the end of Chapter 6." Contrast this with a rigorous application lesson, which might ask students to use $F = ma$ to predict the acceleration of a real object that has been dropped from a certain height.

Because application introduces students to thinking skills that help them move beyond a surface understanding of content, it is important to design lessons and activities that provide students with direct instruction and both guided and independent practice focused on those thinking skills. Not only must you teach students how to apply the concepts and skills they've learned about, you must help them learn how to choose the appropriate thinking skill and be able to explain their reasoning behind that choice.

GUIDELINES FOR RIGOROUS APPLICATION LESSONS

You can promote rigorous application of concepts and skills in four ways.

Teach the Thinking Skill Associated with the New Learning

This might be *cause and effect, compare and contrast, classification, inductive reasoning, deductive reasoning, abstraction, error analysis,* or *evaluation.* You want to give explicit instruction on what each thinking skill is, how the skill can be used, and why someone might need to apply it. Then, provide students with several guided practice activities on using the thinking skill with the content. Take time to structure specific lessons that teach the skill and explicitly ask students to apply the skill to the content.

Cue Students to Use the Thinking Skill

Even after you have taught students how to apply a certain thinking skill to their new knowledge, it will take them a while before they use that skill spontaneously. Early in the process, they may focus more on completing assignments than they do on thinking about what they have learned. You can help students get in the habit of applying thinking skills to their learning by structuring assignments so that they prompt students to consciously apply a thinking skill. For instance, instead of simply asking students to read a chapter in their history texts for homework, give students a guiding question such as "Tonight as you read, pay attention to the effects that new technologies such as the cotton gin had on the cotton trade. What might be the long-term effects of such changes on the slave trade?" Or, to prompt students to think deductively, before students read a poem in class you might say, "This is a sonnet. Based on what we know about sonnets, what can we already predict about this poem?"

Provide Practice Using the New Learning and Associated Thinking Skill

Students need to internalize skills and concepts before they can use them with relative ease. Set some practice tasks to allow students to develop proficiency and fluency with the thinking skill and use it to solve problems. For example, when teaching students about abstracting, you might have them examine a picture of a suitcase with various items, such as a tennis racket, a copy of *Sports Illustrated*, shorts, tennis shoes, polo shirts, and a bottle of aspirin, and have students come up with a list of characteristics of the person who packed the bag and the purpose of the trip. In this way, students can practice the skill of abstracting without also getting bogged down in trying to understand fairly new content. Then, as students begin to understand the skill of abstracting, you can move to practice tasks that are more related to your content. Developing fluency in using a particular thinking skill will help students move to assimilation later.

Promote Metacognition

The point here is to help students monitor their own learning and choose appropriate thinking skills, given a specific instructional context. Teach them to how to ask and answer the following questions:

- What am I trying to accomplish?
- What are my constraints? (What am I allowed and not allowed to do?)
- What thinking skill should I use to solve this problem?
- What aspects of the problem should I pay attention to?

- How much energy do I need?
- When is it time to shift to a new thinking skill?
- When do I need to learn something new in order to solve this problem?

INSTRUCTIONAL STRATEGIES FOR APPLICATION

Here are some teaching strategies that help students rigorously apply thinking skills in order to use what they are learning in a meaningful way.

Have Students Solve Interesting Problems

Interesting problems are not algorithmic, and their solutions are not predictable or binary, with a clear right or wrong answer. Instead, interesting problems often involve nuanced concepts and shades of meaning. Students must choose among several available and viable options, each with pros and cons that must be weighed against often conflicting criteria.

Provide Distributed Practice

Once students have learned how to apply knowledge and skills, help them remember and refine these concepts and skills by distributing opportunities to practice them throughout the unit, semester, and year.

Promote Mindful Practice and Reflection

"Mindful practice" goes beyond routine repetition of concepts and skills; it asks students to make a conscious attempt to reflect on what they are doing before, during, and directly after their practice activities. Help students set learning goals for each practice session, which might, for example, include goals for increasing speed ("I want to learn how to complete these addition problems automatically") or accuracy ("I want to be able to write without making grammatical errors").

Once you and your students have agreed on the practice session goals, the next step is to determine the criteria for the practice session. What will constitute a successful practice session? For instance, if students have a speed goal, they might determine that they will complete 10 addition problems in 10 minutes; if students have an accuracy goal, they might determine that they will write a practice paragraph with no grammatical mistakes.

Students begin a mindful practice session by reviewing their goals and criteria. Next, students begin to practice, and as they do so, they check their performance against their criteria and goals and make adjustments as necessary. At the end of their practice session, students compare their performance against their goals and criteria and think about how they engaged in the process. They evaluate themselves on the final criteria as well as on how effective their practice session was in helping them reach their learning goals. Students also think about what adjustments they need to make in order to make future practice sessions more useful (e.g., practice earlier in the day, eat first, play music during the practice to help with their concentration, or spend more time reviewing the criteria).

Model Thinking Strategies

Showing students what different kinds of thinking "looks like" is key to making these processes explicit and clear. There are two easy ways to go about it.

The first is the *think-aloud*. As you demonstrate how to apply a concept or skill, you literally think aloud, verbalizing your thoughts and the decision-making process to construct a model for how students should think through problems on their own. For instance, when helping students learn how to apply what they know about sentence fragments and run-ons to evaluate their own writing, a teacher might say the following:

> Hmm. First let me read the sentence. "I enjoy going to the park it is fun." OK, that doesn't sound quite right. It makes sense, but something is not quite right. Let me read it again. "I enjoy going to the park it is fun." It seems like it is missing something— some sort of punctuation. What does my voice do when I read it aloud, and when do I naturally pause? "I enjoy going to the park (pause) it is fun." So I naturally pause after the word "park." That's an indication that I need some sort of punctuation there. Let's see. Was it a long pause or a short pause? I'll read it again. "I enjoy going to the park (long pause) it is fun." A long pause seems natural and right, so I want to put a period here. Now let's see if that makes sense: "I enjoy going to the park. It is fun." Yes, that's better, but am I sure I need a period instead of a comma? If I use a period, it means that I need to have a complete thought before the period. "I enjoy going to the park." Is that a complete thought? Yep. So the period is the right punctuation mark there.

The second way to model thinking practices is to help students create *heuristics*, which are written or visual models of a problem-solving process. After you introduce students to the model for applying a skill or concept, have them work alone or in small groups to create a flowchart or a decision tree that represents a model for application they have just learned. When students are finished, have them compare their models and make adjustments as they see fit. Then ask students to use their models to apply what they have learned, again adjusting and refining their models as they develop fluency, learn shortcuts, or discover alternative ways to apply what they are learning. Doing so will help students develop fully articulated heuristics for the thinking process involved here in the application stage and prepare them to assimilate and adapt these models in the stages ahead.

HOW TO STRUCTURE AN APPLICATION LESSON

Use the following outline as the structure for your application lessons:

1. ***Name the targeted thinking skill.*** You want students to be able to make deliberate choices about the skills they use to solve problems. Explicitly naming the skill you are asking students to use facilitates metacognition later on.

2. ***Explain how to apply the skill and why it is important.*** Model the skill or conduct a think-aloud. The point here is to show students what using the skill looks like and how using the skill facilitates problem solving.

3. ***Highlight the thinking skill's steps.*** You can provide step-by-step instructions or a heuristic, or you can simply post the steps in the classroom. This makes a "hidden" thinking skill explicit and also serves as a reminder for students as they learn how to apply the skill effectively.

4. ***Give tips and coaching pointers.*** This step serves to "transfer" the skill from you (who has just demonstrated it and pointed out the steps) to students, who are about to practice it themselves. It's also a good time to address common misperceptions and point out common mistakes.

5. ***Provide practice opportunities with feedback.*** As students practice the skill, provide frequent feedback to let them know how they are mastering the skill, and give them additional tips and pointers to help them improve their practice.

In the **Sample Application Lesson Plan** on pages 75–76, a high school English teacher is using abstracting as a way to help students examine common conceptions of the American Dream across two different plays. The teacher begins by giving students a lesson on abstracting as a thinking skill and provides students with practice that is not directly related to the text. Then the teacher asks students to apply abstracting to the two plays they have finished reading in class. Notice how the teacher provides students with tips and strategies for applying abstracting to the plays they are working on at the beginning of the lesson. Finally, the teacher asks students to use what they have learned through the abstracting exercise to recognize patterns and themes in other works. This learning experience helps students develop a deeper understanding of theme and the ability to detect theme in new and novel situations.

After you have read the sample application lesson, try your hand at creating one of your own by filling out the **Application Lesson Planning Worksheet** on page 77.

Assimilation

Key Question: How will you help your students synthesize what they are learning?

During the assimilation phase of instruction, students extend and refine their knowledge. Here they learn to integrate information and skills so that they can use them routinely to solve problems, create solutions, formulate new understandings, and deepen existing understandings. At this stage of instruction, teachers work to challenge students' misconceptions, uncover any latent misunderstandings, and short-circuit any tendencies toward rigid, formulaic thinking.

An unrigorous assimilation lesson might ask students to memorize patterns, such as the life cycle of plants, and then make and record observations—perhaps keeping an observation journal of plants growing in the classroom and recording when they move through the life-cycle phases. In contrast, a rigorous assimilation lesson might ask students to observe various plants growing in the classroom and record the changes seen. Next, students would discuss any patterns detected over time and make predictions about whether the same patterns would hold with a different species of plant (deductive reasoning). Finally, students would generate and test hypotheses to investigate whether the patterns they detected are true for just the plants they observed, or if these patterns are true for all plants. In this way, students go beyond simply understanding the information. They now combine all the facts, processes, and thinking skills they have learned throughout the unit to learn something new.

Assimilation teaches students to take the thinking skills that were the focus of the application stage and combine them into purposeful thinking processes. For example, you want students to grasp that they can combine the individual thinking skills of *compare and contrast* and *evaluation* to engage in the process of *decision making*. (For tips on selecting which thinking skill to teach, see **Appendix B**.)

Sample Application Lesson Plan

Application Objective(s)
• Students will examine the common conceptions of the American Dream as expressed by two different playwrights. • Students will find examples of this theme in other genres including novels, movies, television shows, speeches, and poems.

Thinking Skill(s)	Learning Material
• Abstracting	• *Death of a Salesman* (Arthur Miller) • *Fences* (August Wilson) • Abstracting charts and abstracting worksheet

Instructional Strategies		
Direct Instruction: Intro to Thinking Skill 1. Provide list of contents in a fictional suitcase, and ask students to decide which character in the two plays packed the suitcase. 2. Ask student to take notes during an introduction to the concept of abstracting: Key Points: Abstracting helps us detect a common theme and experience across multiple works of literature. In the process we (1) learn something new about each work, (2) gain a deeper understanding of the theme and the questions it raises, and (3) see how the theme can play out in multiple ways.	*Guided Practice:* Tips on Thinking Skill Use 1. Present/have students take notes on these tips for abstracting: • Focus first on main characters. How does the main character develop throughout the play? • Refer to the theme words and your notes for each literary work. • When converting a specific pattern into a general one, swap words referring to specific things with words referring to general things. Practice Activity 2. Break the class into two groups, each focused on a different play. 3. Students use the abstracting worksheet to list the pattern for their play, focusing on how the playwright develops the theme, referring to notes completed during the acquisition stage of the unit.	*Independent Practice:* 1. Students find an example of the theme of the American Dream in another work, from another genre. 2. Students complete an abstracting chart comparing their selected work to one or both of the plays. 3. Students write an essay explaining the theme of the American Dream and how it plays out in multiple works of literature, citing examples from one or both plays and a third work of their choice.

(continued)

Sample Application Lesson Plan (cont.)

Instructional Strategies (cont.)		
Direct Instruction: Steps for Abstracting: • Read a literary work and identify a pattern. • Use the specific pattern to identify a general pattern, typically by rewriting the specific pattern in a general form. • See how the general pattern applies to the second literary work. • Find examples of the general pattern in other genres. 3. Whole class completes an abstracting chart for each suitcase. Students must abstract a general pattern of character traits.	*Guided Practice:* 4. Students convert the specific pattern identified in column one to a general pattern in column two. 5. Turning to the other play, students search for the identified general pattern. 6. Students pair with a partner from the other group to compare the general patterns identified. 7. Pairs write a paragraph explaining the similarities and differences in the general pattern they each detected. 8. Students participate in a whole-class discussion of the pattern within each author's conception of the American Dream. *Ask:* How are these different from our idea of the American Dream?	*Independent Practice:*

Ongoing Assessment Strategies and Plans for Formative Responses
• Abstracting chart from direct instruction practice activity • Abstracting charts from the guided practice activity • Practice paragraphs from learning pairs during the guided practice activity • Feedback during the whole-class discussion

A template for an abstracting chart, mentioned in this sample lesson, is available for download at www.mindstepsinc.com/rigor.

Application Lesson Planning Worksheet

Application Objective(s)		

Thinking Skill(s)	**Learning Materials**	

Instructional Strategies		
Direct Instruction:	*Guided Practice:*	*Independent Practice:*
<u>Intro to Thinking Skill</u>	<u>Tips on Thinking Skill Use</u>	
	<u>Practice Activity</u>	

Ongoing Assessment Strategies and Plans for Formative Responses

GUIDELINES FOR RIGOROUS ASSIMILATION LESSONS

There are several ways to promote assimilation.

Teach Students About Thinking Processes

Reintroduce the thinking skills students learned during the application stage of instruction and explain how they can be combined into thinking processes. Here are a few examples:

Thinking Skills Combination	Resulting Thinking Processes
Compare and contrast + evaluation Classifying + evaluation Analyzing perspectives + compare and contrast Inductive reasoning + evaluation Deductive reasoning + evaluation	Decision making
Deductive reasoning + error analysis + evaluation	Problem solving
Induction + classifying Deductive reasoning + analyzing perspectives Compare and contrast + classifying Analyzing perspectives + abstracting	Investigation
Abstracting + evaluation Abstracting + evaluation + error analysis Analyzing perspectives + error analysis + abstracting	Invention
Abstracting + construct support Compare and contrast + abstracting Construct support + classifying Classifying + deductive reasoning	Hypothesis testing

See **Appendix C** for additional guidance on how to teach thinking processes.

Have Students Practice the Target Thinking Process

This practice should be meaningful. Marzano and colleagues (1992) describe three types tasks that are well suited to this effort:

- *Application-oriented tasks,* which promote learning as a by-product of trying to accomplish something else. Students might learn synthesis writing as they conduct research to prepare for a debate on health care, for example, or they might learn problem solving as they plan an imaginary cross-country trip from Ohio to California in 1830.

- *Long-term tasks that extend over a several lessons*, which give students time to develop and refine their understanding and skills into fully elaborated thinking processes. Here, you might present a problem at the beginning of a unit and have students work to solve the problem throughout the unit, applying their emerging understanding of the unit concepts to develop more nuanced ways to solve the problem. For example, if you were teaching a unit on global warming, students might develop and defend solutions to the problem throughout the course of instruction and end the unit by creating a multimedia presentation that makes the case for their plan to combat global warming.

- *Student-directed tasks*, in which students have control over the construction of the task and the product the task generates. For example, you might have students design experiments to test hypotheses they've generated themselves, or invent their own healthy recipes during a unit on nutrition.

Revisit the Thinking Process over Several Units

You can also foster assimilation by returning to the same targeted thinking processes in multiple units. For instance, you might help students develop their ability to test hypotheses by detecting patterns in key battles and how those battles effect the outcome of wars. Students would start by breaking down the Revolutionary War into key battles and then go on to examine how these battles led to each other and moved the war to its end. In a later unit, students might revisit what they have learned about the key battles in the Revolutionary War and relate that to the key battles in the Civil War, identifying patterns of individual battles that turn the tide of war. Then students would use these patterns to predict what effect specific battles in World War I will have on that war's outcome.

INSTRUCTIONAL STRATEGIES FOR ASSIMILATION LESSONS

Here are some strategies that will focus students on using thinking processes.

Have Students Create Artifacts

Give students a chance to demonstrate understanding through the creation of some artifact—an essay, multimedia presentation, project, or some kind of physical model.

This strategy not only helps students see how the various parts of the unit are coming together but also gives them a way to document their growing understanding and use it in a meaningful way.

Provide Guided Practice

Even though students have had practice at this point with using individual thinking skills, combining those skills into thinking processes will require additional practice. Give students plenty of support and scaffolding initially. Then gradually remove those supports so that they can learn to use these thinking processes on their own. You might even want to give students opportunities to practice using thinking processes on neutral material first, before using them with relevant subject matter.

The key is to develop fluency in using these processes over time by giving students several opportunities to practice them with a variety of content. You don't want students to associate thinking processes with one particular unit; you want students to be able to use these processes routinely with a variety of topics, skills, and concepts.

Provide Real-World Tasks

During assimilation, students begin to see how what they are learning can be useful to them personally and in the real world. Provide students with real-world tasks that help them use what they have learned in a meaningful way. Doing so will help students see the relevance in what they are learning and begin to use the thinking processes they have learned spontaneously and routinely both in school and in their lives.

How to Structure an Assimilation Lesson

When planning a rigorous assimilation lesson, structure your lesson according to the following outline, adapted from guidance provided by Marzano and colleagues (1992).

1. *Introduce the thinking process.* Name it and describe how and when it can be used.

2. *Demonstrate the steps of the process.* You want students to see how the process works, not just hear that it works. Consider using a graphic illustration, such as a flowchart, graphic organizer, or diagram for clarification and future reference.

3. ***Give students guided practice using the process.*** Begin with content that is familiar and interesting but neutral—not directly tied to the subject matter students are learning. In this way, you help students focus on learning the process without being distracted by the content.

4. ***Provide opportunity for reflection on the process's utility.*** You want students to think about how they are using the process and what it allows them to do. Consider using collaborative pairwork or summary point writing.

5. ***Help students refine their use of the process.*** Rubrics and feedback are excellent tools here.

6. ***Give students guided practice with the process using content-specific material.*** Provide students with supports to help them develop fluency using thinking processes and plenty of feedback along the way so that they can refine their thinking processes over time.

7. ***Give students independent practice with feedback.*** As students develop their proficiency using the skill, move to independent practice, continuing to give feedback and provide additional opportunities for reflection and refinement.

Take a look at the **Sample Assimilation Lesson Plan** on page 83. It's a 5th grade math lesson, part of a unit on statistics and graphing, and the standard underlying it is *students will use mathematical modeling/multiple representation to provide a means of presenting, interpreting, communicating, and connecting mathematical information and relationships.* This lesson represents the culminating activity for the unit.

The teacher begins by posing a problem. "Each of you has spent a lot of time learning about statistics in this unit," she says. "You've completed several assignments and quizzes in which you demonstrated your growing understanding of statistics. Now it is time for me to give you a final grade for the unit. Take all the grades you earned this unit, and represent them to me in a graphical format that best illustrates how well you have met our key learning outcomes for the unit. Then, write an essay in which you explain to me what final grade you deserve for this unit, why you deserve the grade, and how the mathematical model and representation you have chosen best represents the progress you have made in this unit."

The lesson she designs helps student integrate several skills they have learned throughout the unit. Students must combine their understanding of the various mathematical models and statistical formats (such as bar graphs, pie charts, scatter plots, and line graphs) with the various thinking skills they have learned such as comparison/ contrast (of the various ways to calculate grades and represent data) with evaluation (of their own performance, each mathematical model, and each of the various ways to represent data) and decide which way works best for them. Students then must justify their answers.

The teacher provides students with some support along the way. She begins with a mini-lesson explaining three different ways students could calculate their grades. She also helps students identify the pros and cons of each method. Then students plug their own scores into each of the three models to determine what model works best for them. Next, students review their notes of the different types of statistical representations and choose the best one for them given their model. Finally, students create a visual representation of their performance for the unit and write a short essay in which they explain and defend their decisions.

Now give assimilation lesson planning a try yourself. Use the **Assimilation Lesson Planning Worksheet** on page 84 to map out an assimilation lesson for an upcoming unit.

Adaptation

Key Question: How will you help your students take what they have learned and apply it to new and novel contexts across disciplines?

During the adaptation stage, students take what they have learned in the other stages of rigorous learning and adapt it to fit new and novel situations. Often as a result of adapting what they have learned, students learn something new. For instance, students might take what they now know about finding the area of a square and a triangle and use it to compute the area of an unfamiliar shape such as an octagon; they might use what they have learned about the effect key battles have on turning the tide of war to design an action plan that will help the class win at the upcoming Field Day.

In each case, students must take what they have learned and apply it to solve a new, novel, and often seemingly unrelated problem. Low-level adaptation lessons ask students to take what they have learned to solve fictional problems. They might, for example, be given a word problem asking them to use what they have learned about determining the area of squares, rectangles, and triangles to figure out how much carpet a fictional character needs to buy in order to cover an oddly shaped room. Rigorous application lessons might ask students to take what they have learned about

Sample Assimilation Lesson

Assimilation Objective(s)
Students will determine the best way to present, interpret, communicate, and connect mathematical information and relationships, given a particular audience and set of data.

Thinking Process	**Learning Materials**
Decision making	<ul><li>Math textbook</li><li>Math notebook</li><li>Student grade sheets</li><li>Decision-making graphic organizer</li></ul>

Instructional Strategies		
Direct Instruction: Intro to Thinking Process Lead a class discussion of decision making, including ways students make decisions every day. Point out that the process is basically the same in each instance. Thinking Process Demo/Neutral Content Practice 1. Distribute a set of scores for two football teams over the last three years and have students average each team's scores. 2. Introduce the decision-making graphic organizer. 3. Have students complete the graphic organizer for each team. 4. Lead whole-class discussion of which team is "better team." Students must use data to support their answers. *Ask:* Does "better" mean having a higher average score? What other data should be considered?	*Guided Practice:* Practice Activity 1. Begin by showing students three ways to calculate grades: straight average, weighted average, mean. 2. Working in small groups, students complete a decision-making graphic organizer to weigh the pros and cons of three methods of grade calculation. 3. Individual students plug their grades into each of the three models and write a short paragraph explaining which model best represents his/her mastery of the unit learning goals.	*Independent Practice:* 1. Students select a grade-calculation model and use it to create graphs representing their progress. 2. Students write an essay in which they <ul><li>Identify their final grade.</li><li>Justify their choice of calculation model.</li><li>Justify their choice of graphic representation.</li><li>Explain how their final grade best represents their mastery of the unit learning goals.</li></ul>3. Peer review of essays 4. Essay revision and submission 5. Final essay (graded)

Ongoing Assessment Strategies and Plans for Formative Responses
<ul><li>Grade calculations and guided-practice paragraphs</li><li>Draft essays and peer-review sheets (which students will use to guide revisions)</li></ul>

Assimilation Lesson Planning Worksheet

Assimilation Objective(s)

Thinking Process	Learning Materials

Instructional Strategies		
Direct Instruction: <u>Intro to Thinking Process</u> <u>Thinking Process Demo/Neutral Content Practice</u>	*Guided Practice:* <u>Practice Activity</u>	*Independent Practice:*

Ongoing Assessment Strategies and Plans for Formative Responses

determining the area of squares, rectangles, and triangles to develop a formula for determining the area of octagons.

Adaptation lessons also help students think creatively. Students learn how to engage intensely in tasks for which the solutions are not immediately apparent. They learn how to solve problems by generating new solutions that often rest just outside the boundaries of their current understanding. Doing so helps students learn to push the limits of their ability by synthesizing knowledge and skills and adapting them to unconventional contexts.

Adaptation is the highest level of rigorous learning because it's the point at which students are creating understanding and solutions on their own. They grapple simultaneously with implied meaning and ambiguity, layered meaning and complexity, and they must enforce order on apparent chaos to make sense of the unknown. The disciplined pursuit of their goals under such uncertain conditions helps students develop what Costa and Kallick (2000) call "habits of mind"—the things that intelligent people do to solve whatever challenging problems they face in life. Students aren't just using what they learn in school to solve contrived problems or complete assignments; they are using their learning to address real problems outside school. The thinking skills and processes and the knowledge and skills they have learned become a part of them, and, as a result, students continue to use these skills for the rest of their lives.

GUIDELINES FOR RIGOROUS ADAPTATION LESSONS

Adaptation is never automatic; it's something you must carefully cultivate as students learn to apply their knowledge, skills, and thinking processes to new and novel contexts. There are several ways to do this.

Show Students How to Define and Analyze Problems

The biggest barrier to adaptation is students' tendency to rush to a convenient solution before they really understand the problem. Model for students how to slow down and analyze a problem, ask the right questions, examine alternative solutions, and look for holes in their own understanding *before* settling on a solution.

Show Students How to Detach Learning from Lesson Context

For many students, the knowledge and skills they learn are so tied to the context in which they learned it that they don't even think about how they might use that knowledge and those skills in other ways. If they learned how to write thesis statements for essays, for example, they may have a hard time developing a thesis in a debate. Or if they learned how to measure area by solving problems in their textbook, they may not think to use the same process when measuring a room in order to install carpet. One way to help students decontextualize is to have them solve multiple realistic problems that are superficially dissimilar but require that students use the same strategies. In doing so, you can eliminate associations between concepts and the irrelevant aspects of contexts, and help students form connections between the concepts and knowledge they are learning and the various contexts to which they could be applied.

Teach the Habits of Mind

Costa and Kallick (2000) have identified 16 habits of mind:

- Persisting
- Thinking and communicating with clarity and precision
- Managing impulsivity
- Gathering data through all senses
- Listening with understanding and empathy
- Creating, imagining, and innovating
- Thinking flexibly
- Responding with wonderment and awe
- Thinking about thinking (metacognition)
- Taking responsible risks
- Striving for accuracy
- Finding humor
- Questioning and posing problems
- Thinking interdependently
- Applying past knowledge to new situations
- Remaining open to continuous learning

Show students how these habits are used, and identify specific situations in which each is useful. (See **Appendix D** for a more detailed description of each habit of mind.)

Provide Opportunities for Real-World Application

When selecting problems to use in your instruction, look for ones that ask students to employ the integrated skills and knowledge they have learned so far and one or more of the habits of mind. Find problems for which there is not one apparent answer, and then give students the tools and space to work through them by themselves and with their classmates.

Give Students Space to Find Their Own Solutions

Don't force a problem-solving process on students; give them space to develop one on their own. Let them play around in the messiness of learning, considering and rejecting various solutions, generating and refining possible ideas. Don't script this part of the learning with checklists and quizzes and the like. The students' job is to grapple with difficult and complex but ultimately fascinating problems; yours is to be there to support, scaffold, and facilitate their growing understanding. If you've taught them well during the other stages of instruction and provide the right kind of support and scaffolding, they'll figure things out for themselves.

INSTRUCTIONAL STRATEGIES FOR ADAPTATION LESSONS

The following teaching strategies can help students take what they have learned and apply it to new and novel contexts.

Set Tasks That Relate to Students' Personal Lives and Goals

At this stage of rigorous instruction, students are learning to take what they have already learned and adapt it to solve new problems. One way to help students meaningfully adapt what they have learned is to ask them to use it to solve problems they are facing in their own lives or to achieve personal goals. Thus, you might show students how the persuasive writing strategies they have learned will help them write better college essays or how the geometry skills they have acquired will help them better lay out and decorate their bedrooms. Find ways to help students see the relevance of what they have learned to their own lives.

Use Socratic Seminars and Debate

Socratic seminars and debates allow students to adapt the range of what they have learned to solve a specific real-world problem. Have students engage in a Socratic seminar about love using the thematic implications of Shakespeare's *Romeo and Juliet* or a debate about the long-term consequences of our current environmental policies as a way of helping them go beyond the specific facts and skills they have learned to how those facts and skills personally impact them and the world they live in.

Reinforce Students' Use of Habits of Mind

As students begin to demonstrate habits of mind in their own thinking, reinforce these habits by explicitly pointing them out. Doing so will help students use these habits mindfully, consistently, and with increasing frequency.

HOW TO STRUCTURE AN ADAPTATION LESSON

Although the adaptation stage of instruction requires that you step back to allow students space to solve real-world problems, you still need to plan the learning experience carefully so that students can work through the process rather than wallow in frustration. Use the following outline to structure your application lessons:

1. ***Introduce and explain adaptation and the habits of mind.*** Point out situations where these skills can be useful both in and outside the classroom, and, if possible, give students concrete examples of the habits and skills in use.

2. ***Ask students to analyze real-world problem solving.*** Here, you want to share examples of people solving real-world problems and have students identify the habits of mind and adaptive skills that were used to solve the problem. Keep a running list of their observations.

3. ***Discuss your running list and look for patterns.*** Prompt students to look for the habits and adaptive skills they see people using over and over. What principles about effective adaptation can be derived from the list?

4. ***Identify a related real-world problem for students to solve.*** This should be a problem that is directly related to the content you have covered in the unit and that requires students to use the skills and processes they have learned in order to solve it. You could choose an actual problem or create a simulated problem that requires students to think in real-world ways.

5. ***Introduce the problem.*** Give the details, parameters, and constraints.

6. ***Lead students in a process to define the problem accurately.*** Ask guiding questions to help them consider alternatives, and lead (or ask them to lead) class discussions that uncover key features of the problem.

7. ***Ask students to come up with an initial strategy for solving the problem.***

8. ***Allow students to work on a solution.*** Give them space to try their strategy, experiment, and refine it, providing nonevaluative coaching feedback throughout the process.

The **Sample Adaptation Lesson Plan** on page 90 comes from a 9th grade government course. It's the culminating activity in a unit that focuses on advocacy at the national, state, and local levels of government. Students have examined various advocacy campaigns over time and have discussed the various methodologies used, the challenges of each campaign, and the successes of each. In this lesson, the teacher introduces the following real-world problem: *Select a problem at the local, state, or national level. Then design an advocacy campaign in response to the problem.*

In this unit, students must compare the various campaigns and advocacy actions they have studied, consider the challenges these actions may face when adapted to a different form of government (e.g., moving from the local to the national level), choose those actions that seem most effective given the type of problem they have identified, and adapt those strategies to the current political climate, the level they want to advocate at (local, state, or national), and new technologies. In the process, students develop the habits of creating, imagining, and innovating; questioning and posing problems; and applying past knowledge to new situations.

Now try using the **Adaptation Lesson Planning Worksheet** on page 91 to map out an adaptation lesson of your own.

✓ CHECKPOINT SUMMARY

Rigorous Learning Experiences MUST
Tie directly to rigorous standards
Lead to rigorous thinking
Promote student interests
Build students' capacity for rigor in a systematic way
Increase the likelihood of excellent performance on the summative assessment

Sample Adaptation Lesson

Adaptation Objective(s)
Students will adapt various forms of advocacy used in the past at the local, state, and national levels to design an advocacy campaign addressing a chosen problem.

Adaptation Principles/Habits of Mind	Learning Materials
• Creating, imagining, and innovating • Questioning and posing problems • Applying past knowledge to new situations	• List of advocacy actions • Project assignment sheet • Project planning graphic organizer • Worksheet: "Advocacy in Action—Choosing the Best Plan" • Project rubric

Instructional Strategies

Direct Instruction:	Guided Practice:	Independent Practice:
Intro to Principles/Habits of Mind 1. Review the 16 habits of mind, emphasizing those relevant to this lesson. 2. Ask student pairs to generate examples of when they have used or seen others use those habits of mind. Example Provision 3. Review the various advocacy campaigns students have studied, and identify the habit of mind the leaders/designers used to create and implement the campaign. 4. Identify other key strategies used in the campaign.	Discussion of Principles/Habits of Mind 1. Socratic seminar using the following guiding questions: • "Look at your list of the habits of mind employed in the various advocacy campaigns we have studied. What patterns do you notice?" • "How did these campaign leaders adapt the habits of mind or other strategies to meet their individual context?" • "How do these strategies look different when employed at the local, state, and national levels?"	Real-World Problem Solving 1. Working individually, students select a real-world problem that concerns them. They determine whether it is best addressed at the local, state, or national level and justify their choice. 2. Students select the advocacy actions they will use in their campaign, justifying their choices. They may adapt one or more actions as necessary. 3. Students design an advocacy campaign to address their selected problem.

Ongoing Assessment Strategies and Plans for Formative Response

• Socratic seminar • Graphic organizers • Campaign rough drafts

Adaptation Lesson Planning Worksheet

Adaptation Objective(s)

Adaptation Principles/Habits of Mind	**Learning Materials**

Instructional Strategies

Direct Instruction:	*Guided Practice:*	*Independent Practice:*
Intro to Principles/Habits of Mind Example Provision	Discussion of Principles/Habits of Mind	Real-World Problem Solving

Ongoing Assessment Strategies and Plans for Formative Response

Putting It All Together

In this chapter you will . . .

- [ ] Use what you have learned throughout this guide to develop a rigorous learning unit.
- [ ] Analyze your learning unit using a set of criteria.
- [ ] Develop a plan for communicating your learning goals to your students effectively.

Time-Saving Tools

You will complete the work in this chapter more quickly if you have the following handy:

- [ ] Your plans for an upcoming unit, including the objectives, the day-to-day plans, and the essential understanding or "big ideas."
- [ ] Any assignments you will give for an upcoming unit.
- [ ] The summative assessment for an upcoming unit.
- [ ] Any curriculum guides for the unit provided by your school or district.

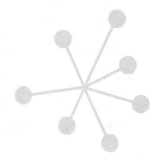

You've spent time thinking through rigorous assessment, content, and instructional strategies. Now it's time to put it all together and create a rigorous learning unit.

So far, we have looked at the various stages in the process of planning rigorous instruction. Now it's time to put it all together to design a rigorous learning unit.

Developing Your Unit Plan

Before we begin, let's review the stages in the process.

TAKE IT STEP BY STEP

How to Plan Highly Rigorous Instruction

1. Create an assessment requiring students to demonstrate the thinking associated with goal mastery and apply learning to real-world or unpredictable situations.
2. Select rigorous learning material that supports goal mastery and possesses the characteristics of rigor that will help students develop necessary thinking skills.
3. Design rigorous learning experiences that help students acquire new information, develop the thinking skills to apply that information, assimilate thinking skills into processes, and apply those processes to new challenges.

Step 1: Create a Rigorous Assessment

The starting point for any rigorous learning unit is to create an assessment that will accurately measure whether students have mastered the learning goals and standards of the unit. Creating the assessment first gives you a chance to clarify learning goals and identify appropriate learning materials and experiences that will best help students meet or exceed the standards. Make the assessment rigorous by asking students to demonstrate the thinking associated with the content, perform tasks that are an extension of the kind of rigorous learning experiences that will make up the unit instruction, and apply what they have learned to real-world or unpredictable situations.

Step 2: Select Rigorous Learning Material

Once you have identified your learning targets, the next step is to select the learning material that will help students reach those targets. Look for material that has implicit meaning, ambiguity, layers, and complexity, as these characteristics will support rigorous learning and the development of thinking skills. If you don't have a choice in the material you use, look for ways to add these elements to the material you have to make it more rigorous.

Step 3: Design Rigorous Learning Experiences

Rigorous learning experiences help students systematically build their capacity for rigor. Start by helping students acquire new information. Next, help students develop the thinking skills they need to apply what they have learned. Once students have a basic understanding of both the material and the thinking skills required by the material, teach them how to assimilate those skills into thinking processes. Finally, show students how to adapt their thinking processes to solve novel problems and develop habits of mind that extend beyond the unit and even beyond the classroom.

Critical Caveats for Unit Planning

As you follow the steps to planning rigorous learning units, here are a few important caveats to keep in mind.

Every Unit Should at Least Reach Assimilation

Not every unit you plan will get students to the point of adaptation. However, in order to ensure that your students have reached highly rigorous thinking and learning, every lesson you plan should at least reach the assimilation level. There are several reasons why.

First, although acquisition and application help students develop the foundational skills of rigorous thinking, both these stages focus on teaching students discrete skills rather than showing students how to synthesize their skills so that they can use them routinely to solve problems. It isn't until a lesson reaches assimilation that students are being asked to integrate multiple skills and knowledge and systematically make meaning for themselves.

Second, if your units don't regularly reach the level of assimilation, you will seriously handicap your students' ability to perform well on standardized tests. The newer editions of state tests and the Advanced Placement and International Baccalaureate exams demand that students synthesize multiple sources of data and demonstrate that they can use thinking processes to solve problems. Preparing students for these tests requires us to teach students how to assimilate what they have learned.

Third, assimilation prepares students to grapple with perplexing unknowns they will face in life outside school. The thinking processes they master during this stage will help them grapple with uncertainty, solve problems, and make good decisions—all key skills they will need to thrive in 21st century society and in the changing workplace.

Plan for Thinking, Not Just Doing

Rigorous unit plans don't just focus on what you and your students will be doing; they also focus on what thinking processes students will engage in. Going beyond the identification of rigorous activities and assignments to focus on the kind of thinking you want those activities and assignments to promote allows you to make stronger instructional choices. This kind of planning also opens up possibilities for differentiation because you are focused on both the final product *and* the process by which students arrive at the final product. When you focus on thinking, you have many more options for how students will develop thinking processes than you do if you simply focus on specific assignments.

To ensure that you are planning each unit with thinking in mind, look at the standards of your curriculum and try detect the underlying learning goal of the standard. What is it asking students to do? Consider, for example, a standard that says *students will analyze past and present trends in human migration and cultural interaction as they are influenced by social, economic, political, and environmental factors*. Remembering our caveat that every unit must at least reach the assimilation level of rigorous learning, you might look at the chart in **Appendix C** and use the reflection questions there to decide that your students need to be able to analyze past and present trends and develop a hypothesis about how human migration trends and cultural interactions are influenced by social, economic, political, and environmental factors. In that case, the thinking process associated with this learning goal is *hypothesis testing*.

With this learning goal clear, you can determine the application learning goals for the thinking skills that go into hypothesis testing, such as finding, identifying, and explaining general patterns in specific information and situations (*abstracting*), and building a case for assertions by providing evidence, proof, or logical arguments (*constructing support*). Therefore, during your acquisition lessons, you will need to help students organize information in a way that will facilitate abstracting, constructing support, and hypothesis testing.

If you wanted to move your students beyond assimilation to adaptation, you could use the chart in **Appendix D** to select the habits of mind that best facilitate hypothesis testing, such as *questioning and posing problems*, and *thinking flexibly*. (You can find charts to help you map learning goals to specific instructional approaches in **Appendixes B–D**.)

Provide an Assessment at Every Stage

In order to determine whether students have reached the level of rigorous learning you are trying to help them reach and are ready to move to the next stage of rigorous learning, you need to include some form of ongoing assessment. These assessments may take traditional forms, such as quizzes and tests, or they may be somewhat less formal, such as homework or in-class assignments, projects, and papers completed during the independent practice phases of lessons.

Because every unit should at least reach the point of assimilation, wait until you have reached assimilation before assessing students in a summative manner. Once you do reach assimilation, it is wise to include both ongoing assessments and a summative assessment that measures how well students have mastered the material, skills, and thinking involved in the unit. Even if your unit goes beyond assimilation to adaptation, a good rule of thumb is to situate your summative assessment at the assimilation stage, since assimilation lends itself particularly well to traditional summative assessments such as tests and essays. Less traditional summative assessments, such as portfolios, capstone experiences, or projects, work best at the adaptation stage.

Use Learning Goals to Ensure Objectives That Are Measurable, Manageable, Meaningful, and Focused on Mastery

Once you have identified your overall learning goals, the next step is to determine how you will help students achieve these goals. One way is to develop individual objectives based on your learning goals for each stage of the rigorous learning process. Again, you can use **Appendixes B–D** to guide your work. In order to write truly rigorous learning objectives, keep in mind four criteria:

- *Measurable:* The only way that you will know whether students have met the learning objectives at each stage and are ready to move to the next stage is to measure the objective through ongoing assessment. Therefore, you need to make sure that your objectives are measurable in some way. As you are writing the objective, determine how you will measure it. If it cannot be measured, you will need to rewrite it until it can be.

- *Manageable:* Sometimes our objectives are so big that it's impossible to achieve them within a single unit. As you write objectives for your unit, think about how long it will take you and your students to meet these objectives. Make sure that your objectives can be accomplished in the time allotted. Otherwise, break up your objectives across several units.

- *Meaningful:* Objectives are meaningful when they allow students to use what they are learning to move to higher stages of rigor. That is why it is so important to focus objectives not on specific tasks (especially when it is unclear how a specific task will help students develop rigorous thinking) but on how students will think. Objectives focused on how students will think are meaningful; objectives focused on tasks are not.

- *Focused on mastery:* Learning objectives should be focused on what students will master at each stage. What will students be able to do and how will students be able to think at the end of that stage of the unit? If your objectives are not focused on mastery, it will be difficult to select appropriate material and learning experiences because you are not clear about where you want students to end up. Keep in mind that mastery is not a single point of success; it represents a range of successful behaviors and thinking. Thus, it is important that you also establish a mastery threshold, or a baseline level of mastery. Think not just about what students will be able to do and how they will be able to think by the end of the unit, but about what the minimal level of acceptable mastery will be. (For more on establishing mastery thresholds, see *How to Support Struggling Students*, another guide in this series.)

Appendix E provides a complete example of a rigorous unit plan.

Now, it's time to use the **Rigorous Unit Plan Template** beginning on page 99 to help you turn all of the information you have captured in this guide's worksheets into a rigorous unit plan for a specific unit you teach.

Teaching for Transfer

To help students move from one stage of rigorous learning to the next, it is important to teach for transfer. *Transfer* is the process of extending knowledge acquired in one context to other contexts. It's because teachers too often fail to teach for transfer that so many students see the facts and skills they learn in school as applicable only within the context of a classroom—and only for the purpose of passing tests or getting good grades. Failure to teach for transfer is why students who learn how to analyze prose during seatwork and tests in class do not take those same analytic skills to critically examine what a political candidate says in a stump speech. It's why students who learn how to dribble a ball during drills in class cannot dribble the ball during a basketball game.

In order to help students transfer what they learn during the acquisition and application stages of instruction to real-world problems, we need to actively and deliberately sever the links between what they learned and the context in which they learned it. Next, we need to show students how the skill is useful in other contexts and how the knowledge or skill can help students achieve their goals. The more we actively teach for transfer, the more students will deepen their understanding of a skill and use it in new and novel contexts.

Rigorous Unit Plan Template

Unit Title

Learning Standards/Objectives

Acquisition Objective(s):	
Application Objective(s):	
Assimilation Objective(s):	
Adaptation Objective(s):	

Learning Materials

(continued)

Rigorous Unit Plan Template (cont.)

	Direct Instruction	Guided Practice	Independent Practice	Ongoing Assessment
Acquisition (use the worksheet on page 64)	**Organizing Strategies:**			
	Direct Instruction	Guided Practice	Independent Practice	Ongoing Assessment
Application (use the worksheet on page 77)	**Thinking Skills:**			

Assimilation (use the worksheet on page 84)	**Thinking Process:**			
Adaptation (use the worksheet on page 91)	**Habits of Mind:**			
Summative Assessment (use the worksheet on pages 33–34)				

Evaluate Your Unit Plan

You've created your unit plan. Congratulations! But you're not done yet. Now you need to check to see if your unit is truly rigorous. Use the checklist on the following page to evaluate how well it meets the criteria for rigorous instruction.

Evaluative Checklist for a Rigorous Unit

You know your unit is rigorous when . . .

You have created learning goals that
- ☐ Map a pathway toward rigorously meeting or exceeding the standard.
- ☐ Specifically outline what students must know and be able to do.
- ☐ Contain a mastery threshold.

You have designed a summative assessment that
- ☐ Makes thinking visible.
- ☐ Asks students to demonstrate what they are learning by solving interesting problems.

You have chosen rigorous learning material that
- ☐ Has implicit meaning, ambiguity, layers, or complexity.
- ☐ Asks students to make meaning for themselves.
- ☐ Creates a space between what students know and can do and what they must know and do.
- ☐ Provides support to help students cross the distance between what they know already and what they must learn.
- ☐ Is within but at the outer edge of students' ability to comprehend on their own.

You have selected rigorous instructional strategies that
- ☐ Challenge students to use what they are learning in a meaningful way.
- ☐ Build students' capacity for rigor from acquisition through adaptation.
- ☐ Help students make connections between what they are doing and the learning goals.
- ☐ Allow your students to take responsibility for the work.
- ☐ Allow you to spend the majority of your time coaching, facilitating, conferencing, and leading learning.
- ☐ Allow students to work in a variety of formats best suited for the type of learning that they are engaged in.
- ☐ Challenge students' misconceptions and help students resist rigid thinking.
- ☐ Help students build their capacity for rigorous thinking, tolerate uncertainty, and work their way through the messiness of learning.
- ☐ Build knowledge into thinking skills into thinking processes into habits of mind.

You have communicated the learning objectives in a way that
- ☐ Allows you and your students to regularly discuss and reflect on the learning goals.
- ☐ Helps your students be able to explain why they are doing what they are doing.

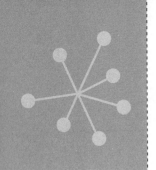

Conclusion

Planning rigorous instruction is itself a highly rigorous process. It requires you to think strategically about where you want your students to go and carefully map the steps to get them there. As you plan rigorous learning units in your own classroom, here are a few final tips and caveats to keep in mind.

- ***Rigorous learning is hard work.*** It can be tempting to sugarcoat how challenging rigorous learning can be. Instead of trying to convince students that mastering the subject matter is easy, just tell the truth. Convey the message that yes, this is hard, but you believe they can do it. Developing and communicating high expectations is another aspect of being a master teacher.

- ***Rigorous learning may lead to some pushback.*** Keep in mind that rigorous thinking and learning is often difficult for students, especially those who have never been asked to think and learn in a rigorous way before. Expect that some students will resist your efforts to expose them to more rigorous ways of learning, and be prepared for some opposition from parents and even colleagues as you introduce more rigor into your course. Help them understand why rigor is valuable, and show them how it will help students both in and outside school.

- ***Rigorous learning must be monitored and supported.*** It is important to give students space to solve problems on their own, but that doesn't mean that you can leave students to struggle unproductively and become frustrated.

You can ease the intellectual shock of rigorous learning experiences for students unused to thinking and learning in highly rigorous ways through proactive support and careful scaffolding. (For more on how to do this, see *How to Support Struggling Students,* another guide in this series.)

- ***Rigorous learning requires a balance between perceived challenges and perceived skills.*** It's students' perception here that is important, not the objective reality. They must believe that they have the skills to meet the challenge. If students' perception of the challenge exceeds their perception of their skills, they become anxious. If their perception of their skills exceeds their perception of the challenge, they become bored.

- ***Rigorous learning does not always proceed in a set, orderly fashion . . . and neither will its planning.*** Even though you may begin your planning by creating your unit assessment, you may need to go back and revise it as you consider various learning materials and make choices about the learning experiences you will provide for your students. Planning assessments first gives you a logical place to start, but you will likely return to your assessment before it's all over to add a question, remove an item, tweak the directions, or adjust the material as you develop a deeper understanding of the unit and how students will progress through it. And if you use formative assessment, you will also be adjusting both learning-material choices and lesson plans and activities in order to provide more effective instruction and help all students reach mastery.

- ***Rigorous learning will take root only when students can see a direct connection between their effort and its payoff.*** You must design learning experiences so that there is a clear connection between what students are doing and the unit's goals. How will completing the lessons and activities in this unit help students reach the learning goals? How will completing this unit help students develop competence? If you cannot answer this question, students will not engage in the work in a meaningful way.

Rigorous instruction lies at the heart of the master teacher mindset articulated in *Never Work Harder Than Your Students.* It asks students to do the intellectual heavy lifting for themselves and provides them with the support they need to do so. When students successfully engage in rigorous instruction, they go beyond mastering the standards of a course; they learn to think for themselves, and they develop habits of mind that will enrich their lives.

"Knowing where your students are going" is more than a matter of identifying a learning goal; it's about moving beyond prescribed learning goals. It's about you and your students reaching—and reaching for—something more. It's about instruction that is richer and more meaningful. It's about showing students how to think in flexible, robust ways that extend beyond the schoolhouse. It's about exploring the possibilities of your curriculum rather than being confined by its limitations. It's about giving students the education they deserve rather than the one prescribed for them.

It's ironic, but when you think this way about your teaching, you can't *really* say you "know where your students are going." Although you must start with a good idea of where students should be headed and then set their course for that destination, when you teach them in highly rigorous ways, they will often surprise you by going even farther than you've planned. When students learn to think and learn in highly rigorous ways, the sky really is the limit.

Appendixes

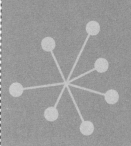

Appendix A: A Guide to Developmentally Appropriate Rigorous Instructional Practices
Methods to Consider Based on the Rigor of the Learning Materials

	Early Elementary	Late Elementary	Middle School	High School
Ambiguity	• Show students how to observe objects from more than one perspective. • Read stories that provide alternative perspectives to favorite stories. • Show students how to develop and explain their own personal viewpoints.	• Introduce the idea that there is not always one answer to a problem, and teach students how to consider alternative perspectives and viewpoints.	• Introduce ambiguous material to students, and teach basic skills for teasing out ambiguity. • Show students how to take a stand and use evidence effectively to defend their choices.	• Show students how to defend, challenge, or qualify ambiguous statements. • Help students understand how to choose effective evidence and support for their choices.
Complexity	• Allow students to play with items that have multiple parts. • Introduce students to concepts and processes with two parts.	• Introduce students to complex material with linear relationships. • Help students identify linear relationships between concepts.	• Show students how to arrange and rearrange skills and concepts in a nonlinear manner. • Teach students how to identify nonlinear relationships among concepts.	• Introduce material with nonlinear, multiple relationships. • Show students how to systematically tease out and grapple with multiple relationships, steps, and concepts.

	Early Elementary	Late Elementary	Middle School	High School
Layers	• Teach students sequence, and show them how to do things in a particular order. • Begin introducing clues to students in sequential order, and help students use those clues to solve small mysteries (think *Dora the Explorer* and *Blue's Clues*).	• Introduce layered material to students, and show them how to engage in systematic inquiry where they use a series of clues or steps to solve a problem or mystery. • Play Sudoku, Clue, and other games where students must systematically shape meaning.	• Show students how to sequentially combine thinking skills in order to develop thinking processes. • Show students how to use those thinking processes to grapple with layered material.	• Ask students to choose and defend thinking processes for working through layered material. • Ask students to experiment with the order of things and examine how doing things out of order changes the outcome.
Implicit Meaning	• Show students hidden object pictures where they have to study the picture to find the hidden object (think *Where's Waldo?*). • Use riddles to help students learn to use context clues to figure out meaning.	• Show students how to use context clues in reading to tease out implicit meaning. • Introduce stories with implied meaning, and teach students specific strategies for discovering meaning for themselves.	• Read poetry and literature with implied meaning, and introduce students to figurative language as a way of uncovering implied meaning. • Introduce students to nonfiction texts with implied meaning, and teach specific strategies for uncovering meaning in prose.	• Introduce Socratic questioning as a way of helping students uncover implied meaning through discussion. • Read opinion pieces and essays where the author's meaning is implied. • Introduce students to rhetorical strategies as a way of uncovering implied meaning.

Methods to Consider Based on the Stage of Rigorous Instruction

	Early Elementary	Late Elementary	Middle School	High School
Acquisition	• Introduce simple graphic organizers to help students organize what they are learning. • Introduce summary-point writing to help students reflect on what they are learning and transfer it to their long-term memories.	• Use graphic organizers to show students how to organize the information they have learned. • Help students learn new facts by focusing on the concepts that underlie the facts rather than mere rote memorization of facts.	• Help students put new learning in conversation with their background knowledge and prior learning. • Help students learn new concepts by making relationships among concepts and ideas explicit.	• Help students shape meaning for themselves by leaving some material unstated. • Help students organize information by pointing out relationships, patterns, and connections to prior learning.
Application	• Show students how to apply what they are learning through games, simulations, and group play. • Name key thinking skills as students use them.	• Introduce students to specific thinking skills and outline the steps to using that skill. • Show students how to apply thinking skills to solve problems, complete work, and improve their own learning process.	• Help students refine thinking skills through practice. • Show students how to shape and refine how they apply thinking skills to develop greater fluency.	• Help students choose and defend their choice of thinking skills to solve real-world, unpredictable problems.

	Early Elementary	Late Elementary	Middle School	High School
Assimilation	• Teach students how to detect patterns. • Give students practice examining concrete materials to detect and predict patterns.	• Introduce thinking processes by combining two thinking skills to solve problems. • Circle back to skills students have learned earlier, and show students how those skills relate to the new skills they are learning.	• Refine thinking processes by practicing combinations of two or more thinking skills to solve real-world but predictable problems. • Teach students how to detect and use relationships and patterns within and among subject matter.	• Extend thinking processes by showing students how to choose and defend their choices of various thinking processes to solve unpredictable problems. • Teach students how to integrate what they have learned in order to create new knowledge.
Adaptation	• Show students how to take something and turn it into something new (e.g., turning a sock into a puppet or turning a story into a song). • Provide students with opportunities to create through art, music, and writing. • Read stories that focus on characters coming up with creative solutions to problems.	• Show students basic problem-solving steps, and begin to introduce one or two unpredictable elements. • Show students how to deal with and work their way out of uncertainty by modeling. • Read stories of how others have dealt with uncertainty. • Introduce habits of mind.	• Ask students to solve problems in unpredictable contexts. Have students reflect on how they adapt their strategy in the face of a new situation. • Introduce real-world problems and give students practice solving them. • Ask students to apply habits of mind intentionally to their work.	• Routinely ask students to solve unpredictable and real-world problems using habits of mind. • Help students refine their adaptive skills through practice and reflection. • Provide capstone experiences that ask students to take on real-world challenges and apply what they have learned to solve these challenges.

Appendix B: A Guide to Selecting Thinking Skills for Rigorous Instruction

Learning Goal	Reflection Question	Thinking Skill
Finding, identifying, and explaining general patterns in specific information and situations	*Is there a pattern or theme in this information?*	Abstraction
Describing reasons for a personal viewpoint as well as the viewpoints of others	*Are there multiple perspectives related to this content?*	Analyzing perspectives
Grouping items or concepts into definable categories on the basis of their attributes	*Can this content be organized into groups?*	Classification
Identifying and articulating similarities and differences among items or concepts	*How are X and Y similar or different?*	Compare and contrast
Building a case for assertions by providing evidence, proof, or logical arguments	*Is there a position that can be defended related to this content?*	Constructing support
Identifying specific examples to support a general statement, rule, or principle	*Are there specific rules that apply to this content?*	Deductive reasoning
Identifying and describing errors in thinking or performance	*Are there errors in thinking or in processes related to this content?*	Error analysis
Inferring unknown generalizations from information or observations	*What conclusions can be drawn from this content?*	Inductive reasoning

Appendix C: A Guide to Teaching Thinking Processes

Learning Goal	Reflection Question	Thinking Skill
Evaluating alternatives to determine a course of action	• *Is there an unresolved decision that needs to be made?* • *Is there an unresolved issue about who or what is best or worst, most or least?*	Decision making
Using knowledge to study perplexing and interesting issues by identifying what is commonly known and accepted, identifying contradictions and confusions, and resolving these contradictions and confusions and then offering and justifying solutions	• *Is there an unresolved issue about the defining characteristics or defining features of something?* • *Is there an unresolved issue about how something occurred?* • *Is there an unresolved issue about why something happened?*	Investigation
Creating something that fills an unmet need or desire	• *Is there a situation that can and should be improved?* • *Is there something new that can be created?*	Invention
Generating and testing explanations of phenomena or events; making predictions based on hypotheses	• *Is there an unexplained phenomenon or historical event for which explanations can be generated and tested?*	Hypothesis testing
Achieving a goal by overcoming obstacles	• *Is there a situation or process that has some major constraint or limiting condition?* • *Is there a situation or process that could be better understood if constraints or limiting conditions were placed on it?*	Problem solving

Appendix D: A Guide to Teaching Habits of Mind

Learning Goal	Reflection Question	Habit of Mind
Sticking to a task until it is completed	*Will this problem require that students sustain a problem-solving process over time?*	Persisting
Using precise language to state a position or support an assertion	*Does this problem require that students use precise language and communicate ideas clearly?*	Thinking and communicating with clarity and precision
Self-imposed delay of gratification	*Will this problem require that students deliberately think it through before arriving at a decision?*	Managing impulsivity
Recognizing and using multiple data sources to solve problems	*Does this problem require students to gather a variety of data sources using multiple senses?*	Gathering data through all senses
Attending to another person's words while monitoring one's own thoughts	*Will this problem require that students consider alternative positions?*	Listening with understanding and empathy
Generating novel and innovative solutions	*Will this problem require that students develop creative or innovative solutions that go beyond the boundaries of perceived limits?*	Creating, imagining, innovating
Being able to shift at will through multiple perceptual positions	*Will this problem require that students consider several points of view or alternatives simultaneously?*	Thinking flexibly
Demonstrating curiosity and engagement in learning tasks	*Does this problem require that students sustain engagement, curiosity, and enjoyment in order to solve it successfully?*	Responding with wonderment and awe
Planning for, reflecting on, and evaluating thinking	*Will this problem require students to monitor and revise their own thinking?*	Thinking about thinking (metacognition)

Learning Goal	Reflection Question	Habit of Mind
Measuring the consequences of making decisions to take responsible risks in the pursuit of a solution	*Does this problem require that students accept confusion and the possibility of failure in order to solve it? Does this problem require that students go against the grain in order to solve it?*	Taking responsible risks
Developing the ability to check over final products for accuracy and make corrections as needed	*Will this problem require students to be precise?*	Striving for accuracy
Detecting and appreciating the inherent humor of situations	*Does this problem contain inherent humor and will students need to detect and appreciate this humor in order to solve it?*	Finding humor
Raising questions that define and shape problems	*Will this problem require that students raise additional questions to understand the problem more fully?*	Questioning and posing problems
Working cooperatively in groups to solve problems	*Does this problem require that students leverage the skills and knowledge of others in order to solve it?*	Thinking interdependently
Making connections between prior knowledge and new learning	*Does this problem require that students access and apply prior knowledge?*	Applying past knowledge to new situations
Striving for continuous improvement and growth	*Does this problem require students to learn and grow continually in order to solve it?*	Remaining open to continuous learning

Appendix E: Sample Rigorous Unit Plan

Unit Title
Grade 9, Unit 4.1 — Trends in Human Migration and Cultural Interaction

Learning Standards/Objectives	
Standard: *Students will analyze past and present trends in human migration and cultural interaction as they are influenced by social, economic, political, and environmental factors.*	
Acquisition Objective(s):	Students will identify past and present trends in human migration and cultural interaction. Students will understand the various social, economic, political, and environmental factors that influenced these trends.
Application Objective(s):	Students will find, identify, and explain general human migration and cultural interaction patterns from specific information and situations (abstracting). Students will use these patterns to build a case for assertions about social, economic, political, and environmental factors that influenced these patterns by providing evidence, proof, or logical arguments (constructing support).
Assimilation Objective(s):	Students will develop and defend hypotheses about the social, economic, political, and environmental factors that influence human migration and cultural interaction (hypothesis testing).
Adaptation Objective(s):	Students will develop habits of mind such as questioning and posing problems and thinking flexibly and adapt these habits of mind to predict future migration trends and cultural interactions based on current social, economic, political, and environmental factors.

Learning Materials

- Textbook (Chapter 10)
- Mitchell & Parks article on migration patterns
- Jenks video series on migration patterns
- World map and individual maps of USA, North America, Africa, Asia, and Europe that illustrate social, economic, political, and environmental boundaries and migration patterns
- Media Center resources (Internet resources, books, and articles on migration and human interaction pulled by Media Specialist for student projects)

	Direct Instruction	**Guided Practice**	**Independent Practice**	**Ongoing Assessment**
Acquisition	**Organizing Strategies:** *Note-taking graphic organizers, summary graphic organizer* • <u>Lecture/note taking</u>: Students listen to and take notes on a lecture on migration trends. • <u>Reading/note taking</u>: Students read Chapter 10 in the text (migration trends influences). • <u>Video/note taking</u>: Students watch a film and take notes on migration trends and the various influential factors. • <u>Mapping activity</u>: Students map migration trends in the USA during several historical periods.	• <u>Small-group summarizing activity</u>: Students use their notes to complete a summary graphic organizer on the various political, economic, social, and environmental factors that influenced specific migration trends. • <u>Class discussion</u>: Using their graphic organizers, students discuss the various migration trends and the factors that influenced them, arguing which factors seem to have had the largest influence on various migration trends.	• <u>Small-group multimedia project</u>: Students select one period of U.S. history and identify the migration trends of that period and the specific political, economic, social, and environmental factors that influenced that trend. Groups create a multimedia display to demonstrate these trends.	• Ticket to leave after class discussion • Open-note quiz after textbook reading • Graphic organizers (graded) • Group projects (graded)
	Direct Instruction	**Guided Practice**	**Independent Practice**	**Ongoing Assessment**
Application	**Thinking Skills:** *Abstracting, constructing support* • <u>Abstracting lesson</u>: Students practice abstracting by looking at trends in popular music, 1960–2010. • <u>Video/note taking</u> • Students watch a film on migration trends in European countries and take notes. • <u>Minilesson and demonstration</u>: What makes effective support?	• <u>Interactive lesson and mapping exercise</u>: Students use their notes to complete an abstracting graphic organizer to abstract specific migration trends in the USA and migration trends in other countries. • <u>Class discussion</u>: What factor does the evidence suggest has had the most influence on human interaction and migration in the USA over time?	• <u>Short essay</u>: Based on the abstracting and evidence exercises, students determine what factor (political, social, environmental, or economic) seems to have the largest influence on migration patterns and write an essay defending their choice.	• Abstracting graphic organizers • Short essays (graded)

(continued)

Sample Rigorous Unit Plan (cont.)

Assimilation	**Thinking Process:** *Hypothesis testing* • <u>Hypothesis testing lesson</u>: Students take notes on the steps to hypothesis testing. • <u>Reading/note taking</u>: Students read and take notes on an article about a specific migration trend in Europe.	• <u>Practice activity</u>: Students practice hypothesis testing in relation to a specific migration trend in Europe.	• <u>Summative assessment</u>: Students select the migration trend that will be the focus of their summative assessment essay, develop and test a hypothesis, outline a defense, and complete the essay.	• Student hypotheses (approved) • Essay outlines (graded) • Essays (graded)
Adaptation	**Habits of Mind:** *Questioning and posing problems, thinking flexibly.* • <u>Minilesson</u>: Students are introduced to each habit of mind and how it is used by historians. Students identify how they use the habits in their own lives.	• <u>Class survey</u>: What factor or factors seemed to be selected by most students as the most influential? Why? What can we infer from this trend? • <u>Class discussion</u>: What factors seem to be exerting the greatest influence on the way that we currently interact in the United States?	• <u>Whole-class discussion/seminar</u>: Based on what we have learned about migration patterns and the factors that influence them, what can we predict about future migration patterns in the USA in the next 50 years? • <u>Practice activity</u>: Students draw a map that illustrates these predictions.	• Maps (graded)

Summative Assessment

Students select and trace a migration trend in the United States, developing and testing a hypothesis about which factor (social, political, economic, or environmental) had the most influence on the migration trend selected.

References

Byrnes, J. (1996). *Cognitive development and learning in instructional contexts.* Boston: Allyn and Bacon.

Costa, A., & Kallick, B. (2000). *Discovering and exploring habits of mind.* Alexandria, VA: ASCD.

Hattie, J. (2009). *Visible learning: A synthesis of over 800 meta-analyses relating to achievement.* New York: Routledge.

International Center for Leadership in Education. (2008). Rigor/relevance framework. Available: http://www.leadered.com/rrr.html

Jackson, R. (2009). *Never work harder than your students and other principles of great teaching.* Alexandria, VA: ASCD.

Marzano, R. (2007). *The art and science of teaching: A comprehensive framework for effective instruction.* Alexandria, VA: ASCD.

Marzano, R., Pickering, D., Arredondo, D., Blackburn, G., Brandt, R., & Moffett, C. (1992). *Dimensions of learning: Teacher's manual.* Alexandria, VA: ASCD.

Marzano, R., Pickering, D. J., & Pollock, J. E. (2001). *Classroom instruction that works: Research-based strategies for increasing student achievement.* Alexandria, VA: ASCD.

Resnick, L. (1987). *Education and learning to think.* Washington, DC: National Academy Press.

Strong, R. W., Silver, H. F., & Perini, M. J. (2001). *Teaching what matters most: Standards and strategies for raising student achievement.* Alexandria, VA: ASCD.

Thompson, M., & Thompson, J. (2009). *Connecting extending thinking: The learning-focused strategies model part 3.* Boone, NC: Learning Focused Solutions.

About the Author

Robyn R. Jackson, PhD, is a former high school teacher and middle school administrator. She is currently the President and Founder of Mindsteps Inc., a professional development firm for teachers and administrators that provides workshops and materials designed to help any teacher reach every student. Dr. Jackson is the author of *Never Work Harder Than Your Students and Other Principles of Great Teaching*, *The Differentiation Workbook*, and *The Instructional Leader's Guide to Strategic Conversations with Teachers*, as well as the how-to guides in the **Mastering the Principles of Great Teaching** series. You can sign up for Dr. Jackson's monthly e-newsletter at www.mindstepsinc.com, follow Dr. Jackson on Twitter at @robyn_mindsteps, or reach her via e-mail at robyn@mindstepsinc.com.

Want More?

Additional resources are available on this book's companion website at www.mindstepsinc. com/rigor. There, you can

- Download copies of the worksheets in this book.
- Find and link to additional free resources.
- Download related video content that provides additional explanations.
- Post your own comments and hear what other readers are saying.
- Sign up to receive a free monthly e-newsletter.
- Explore lots of other reader-only content.

Watch for other books in this series, coming soon.

 Much more about master teachers can be found in this series' companion book, *Never Work Harder Than Your Students and Other Principles of Great Teaching* by Robyn R. Jackson (#109001)